UNLOCK OVER $1K IN FREE BONUSES!

Thank you for your purchase! You've made a powerful decision to change lives and we have the resources to help.

Claim Your Limited-Time Offer Now At:

www.CreditRepairCloud.com/Demo

Get the latest credit repair secrets directly from me!

This is our greatest resource and it's completely FREE!

Subscribe to Credit Repair Business Secrets at:

CreditRepairCloud.com/Podcast

THE ULTIMATE GUIDE TO
STARTING A CREDIT REPAIR BUSINESS

Launch your own profitable business
and start changing lives

By Daniel Rosen
Founder and CEO of
CreditRepairCloud.com

Published by Credit Repair Cloud www.CreditRepairCloud.com

The information in this book is provided for informational purposes only. Neither the publisher nor the author shall be liable for any physical, emotional, financial or commercial damages, including but not limited to special, incidental, consequential, or other damages caused or allegedly caused directly or indirectly, by the information in this book. The author and publisher specifically disclaim any liability incurred from the use or application of the contents of this book. This books offers information, not legal advice. We make every effort to ensure the accuracy of the information and to clearly explain your options. However, we do not provide legal advice (i.e., the application of the law to your individual circumstances). For legal advice, please consult an attorney.

Equifax is a registered trademark of Equifax, Incorporated. Experian is a registered trademark of Information Solutions, Inc. TransUnion is a registered trademark of Trans Union, LLC. FICO is a registered trademark of FICO. Other product and company names mentioned herein are property of their respective owners. No affiliation, sponsorship or endorsement is implied.

Credit Repair Cloud is a registered trademark of Daniel Rosen, Inc.

Library of Congress #1-3325606171
Publisher's Cataloging-in-Publication data
Rosen, Daniel, 1963 —
The Ultimate Guide To Starting A Credit Repair Business /
Daniel Rosen — 1st ed.
p. cm.

BISAC: Business & Economics / Home-based Businesses

ISBN-13: 978-1532898075
ISBN-10: 153289807X

Printed in the United States of America.

First Edition

Contents

How A Credit Repair Business Really Works   55

Credit Dispute Overview   73

Choosing A Dispute Letter   97

Advanced Tactics/Removing Difficult Items   123

Working With Clients 177

The Best Way To Grow Your Business   203

Marketing   211

Your Web Site   221

Scale Faster With Affiliates   231

Credit Repair Cloud, Training & Certification   327

We Change Lives!

19

Introduction

I left home at 13 and made a living by juggling on street corners. That led to a 30 year career in show business; I was a successful comedian, I was on The Tonight Show, I was on Broadway, I was the announcer of The Price is Right. My career was humming along until a bank error devastated my credit, causing a crazy left turn that changed my life forever. I nearly lost my house, I nearly went bankrupt, I nearly lost everything. I was forty years old and I felt like a loser.

I was too broke to hire a credit repair company, so I set out to learn everything I could about credit. The months of letter-writing and record-keeping were overwhelming. I searched for software to help me speed up the process, but there wasn't any. That's when I got a crazy idea to create the world's first credit repair software. My first prototype repaired credit for myself and my best friend, Rick, and it really worked. So I thought; *"Wow, this can help a lot of people!"* So I began adding to it every day, as more people joined our Credit Hero movement. Today, two decades later, that software has grown into "Credit Repair Cloud," the software used by thousands of credit heroes, that has helped millions of people and powers the credit repair industry. Some of our Credit Heroes make millions of dollars a year and they all change a ton of lives.

Credit repair is a great thing; it does a service for your community and its also good karma, because it helps people who are in need. It's an affordable business you can launch with little more than a computer. Since it's a recurring revenue business (with clients paying you monthly), each new client grows your revenue stream — and your profit potential is unlimited. I've written this book because there's no definitive guide for folks wanting to learn this craft and grow their business. My goal is to help you to to become a Credit Hero, to build and grow your own profitable credit repair business and start changing lives.

You got this!

Daniel Rosen, founder of CreditRepairCloud.com

The Secret To Success
in Credit Repair

**IN A HURRY?
STOP AND READ THIS CHAPTER
BEFORE YOU GO ANY FURTHER
WITH YOUR BUSINESS**

The Secret To Success In Credit Repair

As founder of Credit Repair Cloud, I have a great vantage point to see exactly what works to build a successful business. Some companies make millions of dollars and others struggle. This guide will help you be among the former.

Credit Repair does change lives and can make you a millionaire, but it's *not* a get rich quick scheme. It takes dedication and hard work.

I've noticed one common trait in all the companies with the greatest success: they *always* follow the same path of the other successful businesses rather than trying to reinvent the wheel. They keep it simple, they're focused, great with people, honest, transparent, they have an entrepreneurial spirit and they work very hard to keep momentum. They have a big passion for credit, learning new processes, helping people, making a difference in their community, over-delivering value and changing lives. Their passion becomes infectious, it excites their clients and grows their business like wildfire.

I've also noticed a common trait in the people who don't succeed; they're in a hurry, they panic, they don't read instructions, they only focus on money, they look for shortcuts, they're unprofessional, they communicate poorly (usually by texting, if at all), they don't answer their phone, they hide who they are, they waste time and energy on the wrong things, they operate their business in sketchy ways — approaching it like a hustle instead of a service, and they don't make an effort to learn their craft.

There Are No Shortcuts

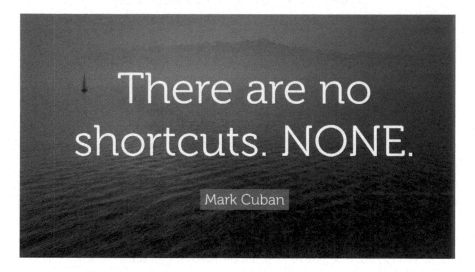

If you're just in a hurry to make money, and don't have patience and passion to grow a business, and a desire to change lives, make an impact and be truly awesome at what you do, stop right now. This business is not for you.

Successful people know that shortcuts aren't real. They understand that you must invest the time to master new skills and processes. They are constantly reading, learning, sharing with others, and they know that launching a successful business means growing slow and overcoming a daily obstacles. They know it's a long journey and they accept the challenges to make that journey fun.

12 Steps To Grow From Zero To A Million Dollar Credit Repair Business

At our annual conference, we give awards to the Credit Heroes who have earned a million dollars in our software, Credit Repair Cloud. This is so exciting for us to see this living proof of the lives we've changed. Many of them have started from zero with no budget, some were homeless, sleeping in cars, yet they learn overtime to leverage one success into another. For example, you may not have a budget for advertising or assistants just yet, but don't worry. You don't need to gamble on any of that if you're just starting out. Get them later when you can afford them with your profits. This is called "bootstrapping."

Here are the steps to bootstrap a highly profitable credit repair business from nothing.

1. Learn the flow of Credit Repair Cloud Software and practice the steps first with your sample client and sample report (in CRC), so you know it like the back of your hand. Repeat this mantra: "Import, audit, tag and save." If you don't know what this means yet, don't worry, you will soon when you follow the chart in the later chapter "The recipe for a profitable credit repair business."

2. Be your own first client and work on your own credit. Continue to follow the steps in the chart and follow its flow. Go slow, only dispute a handful of items and wait for results. Never dispute a ton of things all at once — unless you were a victim of identity theft and have a police report to include with your letters.

3. Offer to help family and friends (for free). Learn to import a report, run a free credit audit, give an awesome client consultation, tase and save the report and create their round 1 letters. Don't dispute too many items at one time if you're just starting. Practice slowly and methodically with those test clients and get your processes down.

4. 30 days later, you will start to have positive results. Get testimonials and videos that show their success and post them online (Facebook, etc). Real excitement from real people whose lives you've changed will become the "social proof" that will sell your services for you. It's free and it will begin to grow your business organically. Happy clients are your best advertising, so offer friends and family (happy clients with results) a commission for each "paid client" that they refer to you.

5. Before you start to charge money for credit repair, make sure you are compliant. Each state has different rules, so do your due diligence. Some states require a bond, others don't. We cannot give you legal advice, so check with your state or an attorney. This is all part of the process with any business; little hurdles to jump over. See the "business checklist" later in this book.

6. Create a very simple business with simple consistent pricing. Charge every client the same affordable recurring monthly fee. Deliver results, educate clients, give away information, show value, have a full refund policy for people who are not happy, be amazing and grow an awesome reputation.

7. Not getting results? Get more education. If you're a Credit Repair Cloud user, join our private Facebook community to network with successful credit repair pro's who have already been in your shoes, take our Credit Hero Challenge, take our other courses, read as many books as you can, come to our conferences and never stop learning. Your clients see you as the expert. Become that expert.

8. Print some business cards and flyers that advertise your services. These are inexpensive. If you can afford it, get some brochures.

These are your tools, so make them look awesome. We have templates for these for our paid users and you can also hire inexpensive artists on sites like Fiverr.com.

9. Build relationships with financial professionals (mortgage brokers, realtors, auto dealers, tax preparer, etc.) to become your affiliates and you'll pay them for each "paid client" they refer to you.

10. Grow your mail list by giving away ebooks, guides and valuable articles. Build multiple drip email campaigns for potential clients, new clients and affiliates. Write articles and emails that are entertaining, motivating and informative. They should never look like ads.

11. Later, as your budget grows, invest in assistants and a marketing team and begin to delegate the busywork. This will free you up to just concentrate on being awesome, building more professional relationships and getting more clients.

12. Do whatever you can to keep your passion, your momentum and your excitement for what you do. Learn from mistakes they help you to grow. Don't make money the goal. Celebrate small successes, be proud and enjoy the journey. As success comes, give back and help others as much as you can. This will grow your business larger than your wildest dreams.

We see people start businesses on a shoestring in exactly this way and become millionaires. If you visit our site, you'll see their stories. If you come to our Credit Repair Expo conference you'll meet them. It's proven system and it really works, but you must be patient and learn your craft.

This book has great information to help keep you on your path and focused. Everyone has their own idea of how to run a business, but the ideas I've written here are from my experience of watching credit repair businesses for over a decade, all day, every day, seeing what works and what doesn't.

Let's be clear. Credit repair is not a "get rich quick" scheme. Starting any business takes hard work. It will feel like pushing a boulder up a cliff, but if you keep positive, have passion and do at least one thing every day to move your business forward, you will always have momentum.

Building a business is like building a house. There are many parts to be planned — but you must lay the foundation first.

The goal of this book is to explain all the parts of the foundation, so you can put them all together and build your profitable business. If you're ever lost on this journey, come back and read this chapter or take some of our courses. They are all affordable and many of them are even free.

My recommendation is to start with the **CreditHeroChallenge.com**.

I also recommend that you join our Facebook Community, to network with thousands of credit repair professionals who love to share advice, answer questions and share resources. It's one of our greatest resources and we highly recommend it. Apply for free at **https://www.facebook.com/groups/creditrepaircloudcommunity**

The Secret To Wealth

Yes, There Is A Secret To Wealth

I'm a multi-millionaire today, but my path to getting here wasn't all rosy. I come from nothing. My family didn't have money. I didn't finish high school. I left home at 13, and I was homeless. Everything I've ever achieved in life has come from hard work and learning from failure. I've realized that my next stage in life is about giving back, so I've written this book to share my secrets with you. If you follow them, you won't have to work as hard as I did, so I've broken it all down into easy to follow steps.

So before any further discussion about credit repair, let's talk about the secret to wealth

When you work a normal job, you get paid by the hour or by the task. You'll never get rich that way. You're making someone else rich…

The secret to wealth is making money while you sleep…

How can such a thing be true? Read on, grasshopper…

How Do You Make Money While You Sleep?

Recurring revenue! Here's the recipe…

- Charge a monthly recurring fee: It must be affordable
- Keep your clients happy and give value (so they continue to pay)
- And then to grow it, just add a few more clients every month

It really is that simple. You do that and your revenue will grow <u>larger</u> every month. It will start to look like this…

Since it only takes a few minutes of work per client per month, and those clients each pay you monthly, the goal is to add as many happy paying clients as you can. Just 100 clients paying you $99 a month is $9,900 in revenue *every month*. Have 1,000 clients at that rate and your monthly revenue will $99,000 per month.

We have some software users who have thousands of clients and make close to a million dollars a month. Here's how they <u>all</u> started…

- They repaired their own credit and got great results
- They repaired credit for family and friends and got great results
- This brought referrals and real paying clients
- By giving awesome customer service, their word of mouth grew
- When the client list got bigger, they hired an assistants
- They increased referrals by building relationships with affiliates

This is a gratifying business, because it helps people and changes lives — and earning a nice, comfortable living is an awesome benefit.

Credit Repair Training And Certification

A wise man said, *"You've got to know the business before you can grow the business."*

Visit our Credit Hero Challenge for an online course with live training and mentorship. You'll learn how to repair your own credit and then turn it into a lucrative business that helps others and changes lives. You'll get your first clients, you'll get your processes down, you'll receive 3 certifications, you'll have a lot of fun, and you'll gain confidence with a solid foundation to launch your new business.

Best of all, it costs less than you'll spend to tale your family to McDonald's for dinner. Signup at **CreditHeroChallenge.com**

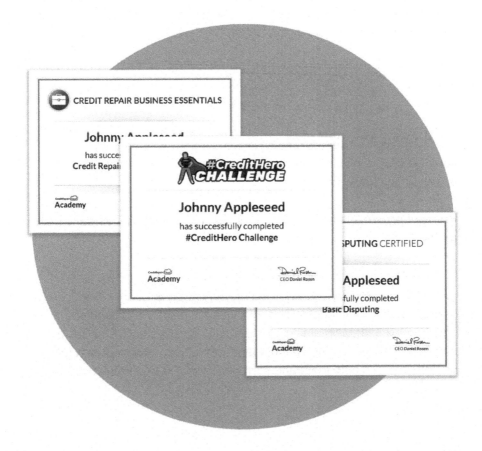

Why Start A Credit Repair Business?

Over 100 million Americans have poor credit. Most don't understand the credit reporting system and will gladly pay good money for someone to help improve their credit. *Why shouldn't that be you?*

Credit repair is a low cost startup. The three main ingredients you'll need are a computer, a desire to help people and a good personality (since this is a people business).

Unfortunately for consumers (and fortunately for you), the credit reporting system is designed to hurt people. It was devised by the banks as a way to keep people poor. Once you fall behind it becomes nearly impossible to recover. This is no accident. If you're late on a payment they can raise your interest rate, making it even harder to pay the debt off. They lower your credit score in the process, increasing interest rates on your other accounts. This is how banks get richer.

To make things worse, they make a lot of mistakes! In fact, *most* credit reports have mistakes. The system is horribly flawed. Thankfully, there is something you can do. You, as a consumer, do have the right to dispute negative items on your credit report. Even accurate items can often be removed. You just need to know the rules. Once you learn this system, you'll be able to help others and use this skill to start a business or to enhance an existing business.

A credit repair business is one business that will always earn a profit.

Even in the most troubling economy, a credit restoration business will succeed and prosper. Here is a fact: nearly eight out of ten Americans struggle with their finances. This very quickly takes a toll on their creditworthiness. Maintaining good credit is a necessity in our society and during troubling times people tend to rack up more debt and fall behind. You can help them and earn good income in the process.

A Credit Repair Business

- Is recession-proof

- Excels during tough economic times

- Is easy to run from your home

- Needs no degree

- Can make you money immediately

- Has recurring revenue and scales quickly

- Is easy to start with very little investment

- Is a great supplement to your existing business and clients

- Creates passive income

- Does a service for your community

Learning the basics of credit repair will enable you to start a new business immediately. Helping others repair their credit history and have a fresh, new head start on life is extremely rewarding. While it's true that consumers can do this very same work themselves, most are afraid or lack the skills to communicate with credit bureaus and negotiate with creditors. This is where you come in to help. With the right tools, you can take away your client's credit pain by navigating the credit repair process for them. So let's get started!

What Does A Credit Repair Business Really Do?

See the next page for a super-simple overview of what a credit repair business does and how it becomes highly profitable. Credit Repair Cloud reduces the work to a few minutes per month per client. The recipe is simple: Be awesome so your existing clients will love you and keep paying your monthly fee. Then each month add just a few more paying clients. With the simple flow (as illustrated on the next page) your revenue will continue to grow *larger* each month. Voilà! The power of scalable recurring revenue!

The Recipe For A Profitable Credit Repair Business

10 Steps To A Profitable Credit Repair Business

with **CreditRepair** (Cloud)

 1 **You've got a new lead**

A new lead appears in your CRC from your site or an affiliate. You invite them to a "Free Consbultation and Credit Audit."

 2 **Start the free consultation**

Instruct the lead (potential client) to sign up for your preferred credit monitoring provider to get all 3 reports and scores for $1.

 3 **Client shares login details**

Potential client shares login details with you, so you can import the report into CRC. Explain importance of keeping the credit monitoring active.

 6 **New client onboarding**

Client logs into her portal, signs your agreement, watches a video about your process and uploads a photo of her drivers license and a utility bill with her smartphone.

 5 **Convert to client**

Complete the client's profile, change status from "lead" to "client" which sends portal login details to the client.

 4 **Import & run credit audit**

You import the report and run Simple Audit. A credit analysis report wows the client and explains your services. It's your greatest sales tool ever.

7 **Review & tag pending report**

View the pending report, where CRC has analyzed and flagged the negative items. Tag each item with a Reason and and Instruction, and save your work. You've just planned the entire lifecycle of this client.

 8 **Run the dispute wizard**

Run Wizard to add up to 5 items to dispute letters. Send to all 3 bureaus with copy of client's photo ID and utility bill. Wait 30 days for bureaus to respond. Update changes in CRC. Repeat with 5 new items each month.

 9 **Lather, rinse & repeat**

If a bureau claims an item is verified, challenge with a new letter. Items are often removed, client sees results, continues to pay your monthly fee and tells her friends.

10 Once you've nailed the basics, it's time to grow and scale!

 Grow your business faster by building relationships with affiliates. Pay them a commission for each "paid" client they refer to you.

 Offer a money back guarantee. Concentrate on being awesome and giving value. Educate your clients and collect testimonials.

 Each month add a few more paying clients and your revenue will always grow larger.

Here are these steps broken down:

This is the flow of a successful Credit Repair Business in Credit Repair Cloud. You'll want to practice this again and again until it's in your DNA, first with Sample Client, then yourself, then family and friends, and finally with real paying clients and grow it into a million dollar business.

1. **You get a new lead!**
   A new lead appears in your CRC from your site or an affiliate. You invite them for a "free consultation and credit audit."

2. **Start the free consultation**
   Instruct the lead (potential client) to sign up for your preferred credit monitoring provider to get all 3 reports and scores for $1.

3. **Client shares login details**
   Potential client shares login details with you, so you can import the report into CRC. Explain importance of keeping the credit monitoring active.

4. **Import & run credit audit**
   You import the report and run Simple Audit. A credit analysis report wows the client and explains your services. It's your greatest sales tool ever.

5. **Convert to client**
   You close the deal, change the Lead to a Client, complete their profile, and click save, which sends their portal login details.

6. **New client onboarding**
   Client logs into her portal, signs your agreement, watches a video about your process and uploads a photo of her drivers license and a utility bill with her smartphone

7. **Review & tag the pending report**
   View the pending report, where CRC has analyzed and flagged the negative items. Tag each item with a Reason and and Instruction, and save your work. You've just planned the entire lifecycle of this client.

8. **Run the dispute wizard**
   Run Wizard to add up to 5 items to dispute letters. Send to all 3 bureaus with copy of client's photo ID and utility bill. Wait 30 days for bureaus to respond. Update changes in CRC. Repeat with 5 new items each month.

9. **Lather, rinse & repeat**
   If a bureau claims an item is verified, challenge with a new letter. Items are often removed, client sees results, continues to pay your monthly fee and tells her friends.

10. **Once you've nailed the basics, it's time to grow and scale!**

   - When a client sees results, capture their excitement with a testimonial. Show the results on your site and in facebook.

   - Offer a commission for each client who refers a friend (as a paying client).

   - Grow your business faster by building relationships with affiliates. Pay them a commission for each "paid" client they refer to you.

   - Offer a money back guarantee. Concentrate on being awesome and giving value and educating your clients.

   - Each month, just add a few more paying clients and your revenue will always grow larger.

   - When you start to grow larger, get an assistant so you can spend more time providing an amazing customer experience and building more professional relationships.

Want To Learn How To Grow A Million Dollar Credit Repair Business?

Take our FREE web training at CreditRepairCloud.com/FreeTraining

Reports And Scores

What Is A Credit Report?

A credit report is a consumer's financial report card. Lenders report their history with you to the credit bureaus, and the credit reports are the summary. It lists the types of credit you use, how long your accounts have been open, and whether you pay your bills on time (among other factors).

Credit card companies, banks, mortgage companies, auto loan and insurance companies, landlords and employers use credit reports to check on your credit history before deciding on doing business with you. Why? They know that if you were responsible in the past, you are likely to be responsible in the future (and vice versa).

What Is Credit Scoring?

"Credit scoring" is a system creditors use to help determine whether to give you credit, and how much to charge you for it. When you apply for credit the creditor or lender will request your report and score from one of the big three bureaus—Equifax, Experian, or TransUnion—and sometimes (for example, when applying for a mortgage) they will pull reports and scores from all three. Your "credit worthiness" comes from calculating your credit history against a system called the Fair Isaac Model. Fair Isaac uses a variety of factors to determine your score: your bill-paying history, the number and type of accounts you have, late payments, collection actions, outstanding debt, and the age of your accounts.

The final outcome of those calculations is referred to as your FICO® score. FICO scores range from 300 to 850, but the majority of scores fall between the 600s and 700s. While a FICO score above 700 will get you a very good mortgage rate a score above 720 will get you an even better rate, saving you thousands of dollars. A score below 700 will make getting a loan very difficult for you and definitely should be improved.

Correcting mistakes on a credit report in order to repair an undesirable credit score takes time and it's your responsibility to correct mistakes that may appear in your credit report. To do this, you must regularly obtain copies of your credit report and contact each of the big three credit reporting bureaus and send dispute letters to correct any misinformation.

What Affects Your Credit Score?

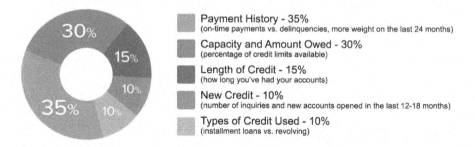

Payment History - 35%
(on-time payments vs. delinquencies, more weight on the last 24 months)

Capacity and Amount Owed - 30%
(percentage of credit limits available)

Length of Credit - 15%
(how long you've had your accounts)

New Credit - 10%
(number of inquiries and new accounts opened in the last 12-18 months)

Types of Credit Used - 10%
(installment loans vs. revolving)

A credit score is a number generated by a mathematical formula that is meant to predict credit worthiness. Credit scores range from 300-850. The higher your score is, the more likely you are to get a loan. The lower your score is, the less likely you are to get a loan. If you have a low credit score and you do manage to get approved for credit then your interest rate will be much higher than someone who had a good credit score and borrowed money. Therefore, having a high credit score can save many thousands of dollars over the life of your mortgage, auto loan, or credit card.

What A Low Credit Score Really Costs You

Your monthly loan and credit card payments can easily be 40% higher with a low score! A higher credit score can save you an enormous amount of money by qualifying you for a lower mortgage interest rate (and by letting you qualify in the first place). According to Fair Isaac (at the time of this writing), lenders would probably demand a 5.5% percent interest rate on a $300,000, 30-year fixed mortgage for a borrower with a credit score between 500 and 579. That's a $1,700 monthly payment for principal and interest. But a score above 760 would qualify you for about a 3.3 percent rate with a payment of $1,300 a month. That's savings of $500 each month, and more than $100,000 over the life of the loan!

This chart illustrates just how much a low credit score can cost you over the life of a loan:

YOUR CREDIT SCORE	*ADDITIONAL COST TO YOU
720+	$0
700-719	$7,000
675-699	$30,100
620-674	$86,450
560-619	$143,640
500-559	$287,200

*Based on a 30 year, $200K loan at 5.6% interest

How Your Credit Score Affects Your Interest Rate:

FICO stands for Fair, Issac & Co. They're the folks who created the mathematical formula used to calculate what is commonly called the FICO score. This three-digit number is a big determinant in whether or not you get a mortgage or any other type of loan. FICO helps banks, credit card issuers, auto loan companies, and other lenders decide if you're a credit risk. The higher your score, the more likely you'll be approved for a mortgage (and the lower your rate will be). Here is the average rate/score breakdown:

YOUR CREDIT SCORE	*INTEREST RATE
720+	6.089%
700-719	6.214%
675-699	6.751%
620-674	7.901%
560-619	8.531%
500-559	9.289%

*Based upon rates at the time of this writing.

As you can see, a credit score of 720 or higher is the magic number to hit. Simply put, a better credit report will raise your credit score. A higher credit score will get you a lower interest rate. The lower your interest rate, the more money you will save.

Don't have perfect credit? No worries. You can improve your own credit while learning this business — and quickly too. You can have negative misinformation wiped away from your reports, lower your payments, and raise your credit score higher to get the loan that you want at the low interest rates you deserve. All it takes is perseverance, a positive attitude, and knowledge.

How Your Credit Score Affects The Cost Of A Car

Brand New Toyota Camry
$23,000 (66 Month Term)

John and Jane have 2 different credit scores and they both want this same car. Here's what it will cost each of them:

John	**Jane**
Credit Score: 730	Credit Score: 599
Interest rate: 1.99%	Interest rate: 14.99%
Payment: $368.22	Payment: $513.97
Total Interest Paid $1302.39	Total Interest Paid $10,921.44
Total payments: **$24,302.39**	Total payments: **$33,921.44**

In this real-life example, Jane pays **$9,616.05 MORE** than John for the exact same car and price! This same thing happens with your credit cards, mortgage, loans, etc. Cleaning up your credit will lower your bills and can save hundreds of thousands of dollars!

Is this making sense? You will use these same examples to educate your clients on the value you bring to their lives. With your help, they will be able to achieve their dreams.

Ordering Credit Reports

The first step with each new client is to obtain fresh new reports from all 3 bureaus. Here are some easy ways to do that:

Getting Credit Reports For Free

The three nationwide consumer reporting companies (Equifax, Experian, and TransUnion) have set up one central service through which you can order your Free Annual Reports. You are eligible for one free credit report per year. If you're not eligible for free reports, the cost to purchase one is up to $10, depending on your state. To order, visit annualcreditreport.com, call (877) 322-8228, or complete the Annual Credit Report Request below and mail it to:

Annual Credit Report Request Service
P.O. Box 105281
Atlanta, GA 30348-5281

Pro tip: Free is nice, but unfortunately, free annual reports do not have scores. For that reason, we don't recommend them for credit repair. Instead, we recommend spending $1 to get all 3 scores in seconds by signing up for credit monitoring.

Getting Reports And Scores For $1 With Credit Monitoring

Credit monitoring is awesome because you can see the reports and scores as they change. Most credit monitoring companies charge $1 for a trial with instant access to all 3 reports and scores (a real bargain). Just be sure you're gaining access to all 3 reports and scores because some companies only give access to one.

The client can certainly cancel the free trial if ongoing credit monitoring is not wanted. But without credit monitoring there is no way to monitor the scores as they change, so we recommend encouraging your client to keep the monitoring service active for as long as they are repairing their credit.

Credit Report Providers change often, so if you're a Credit Repair Cloud user, visit the page in your software that shows the recommended providers that will import into Credit Repair Cloud and will also pay you a commission for each client that signs up. You'll find that by logging into your Credit Repair Cloud and visiting **"My Company>Credit Monitoring Service."**

Can I "Pull" Reports For My Client?

No way, José! The client must always be the one ordering the reports and signing up for credit monitoring. As a credit repair company you're "not authorized" to pull reports, so please don't try to order reports for your client. The credit bureaus will know you're ordering reports for someone else. You can't fool them.

The great news is that when a client orders their own reports, they don't suffer a hit to their soore. Most credit repair companies have the client sign up for credit monitoring and then they ask the client for their login details. Once you have access to the online report, you can log in and import the report source code into your software to begin the process.

Who Orders The Credit Reports?

As discussed earlier, clients must order their own reports — and this self-order doesn't cause a hit on their score.

Per some of the biggest credit repair firms, the best ways to order reports are for the client to sign up for credit report monitoring and send you the login details (and security word if applicable).

As of the writing of this book, Credit Repair Cloud will import online credit reports from several different report providers. Since those companies change periodically, we will list them in the software. They charge $1 for a trial with instant access to all three reports and scores (a real bargain). We recommend encouraging your clients to keep the credit monitoring service, because it's the only way to see updated reports and scores.

If you're a Credit Repair Cloud user, please remember that we are not affiliated with these providers of credit reports: We are only providing this information to be helpful to you. Your client is ordering the reports. We are not a part of that scenario.

When you print and send your Round 1 letters from the Dispute Wizard, be sure to include copies of the client's photo ID and utility bill. And just like that, you just completed the main first work for your client and set up a revenue stream from them. Congrats!

What If My Client Doesn't Want To Pay For Credit Monitoring?

As our friend (and credit repair multi-millionaire) Derrick Harper, Sr. brilliantly wrote:

For clients who don't want to keep credit monitoring, have this conversation with them verbatim, word for word:

"Sir/ma'am, if I was your doctor and I had to do a surgery on your knee, would you prefer me to do it with an X-ray, or without an X-ray?"

Then ask, "what if the X-ray costs a few bucks extra?"

They will still say yes.

Let them know "credit monitoring is the X-ray to your credit."

We love Derrick Harper.

What If Your Client Has Reports From Another Provider Or A PDF?

Yes, no worries. Even if the report you have is not in a format that can be imported into software, all that matters is that you have fresh, current reports and that you've circled the items that you wish to dispute. However, keep in mind, if you have a report that cannot be imported, you'll be doing a lot of work manually and you won't be able to run Simple Audit to create a credit audit report.

You're far better having the client signup for credit monitoring for $1 so you can have reports and scores that will import, so you can wow the client with your amazing tools. Always be sure to remind the client that there is no hit to their score when they are ordering the reports themselves.

Credit Repair Cloud users: Credit Repair Providers come and go, and the ones you see mentioned here may not last as long as this book. So just check the list of current credit report providers, by looking within your Credit Repair Cloud account at "**My Company>Credit Monitoring Service.**"

How Did That Get On My Report?

One of the first questions that your new client might ask is "Where does the information on my credit report come from?"

When starting a credit repair company, being an expert on this type of information will build trust with clients and help grow your business.

There are 3 basic categories of information included in a credit report:

1. **Basic Personal Information:** This is self-explanatory: full name, date of birth, current address, social security number, and employment information, and all places lived.

2. **Collections and Accounts:** This is the information most people think of when discussing a credit report. This is usually separated into two buckets of information: all open lines of credit and all accounts that may be delinquent or in collections.

3. **Public Financial Records:** This can include bankruptcy filings, tax liens, or any court judgments that affect your credit status.

These three categories of information are collected and applied to credit reports via these different methods:

- **Basic personal information** is originally reported by the individual borrower when opening his/her first line of credit. This is updated throughout the borrower's lifetime as new lines of credit are opened.

- **Collections and account information** is updated most frequently and proactively — usually monthly — by collection agencies and lenders directly to the credit bureaus.

- **Public records** are the only pieces of information that are proactively collected by the credit reporting agencies solely for the purpose of reporting.

Credit reporting can be a complicated and confusing topic for those who are not experts in credit repair. As a credit repair professional, you have an opportunity to position yourself as a trusted and knowledgeable advisor in all things credit repair. How credit reports are made and updated is a crucial component that your clients will surely benefit from learning.

Credit Repair Cloud users: When you import a credit report into Credit Repair Cloud, and click to run "Simple Audit" it will analyze that report and highlight all the items that need attention in an awesome Credit Audit Report for your client. That report is your greatest sales tool. At that point you'll go through the report with your client to create a game plan.

How A Credit Repair Business Really Works

What Does A Credit Repair Professional Do?

Credit repair in itself is simple: you send letters for clients who can't be bothered to send them for themselves and teach them how to better manage their credit. For this, they pay you a monthly fee. And if you have software to run your business, it automates the processes and reduces the work to a few minutes per client each month.

Credit Repair Cloud imports the reports, analyzes them, creates instant dispute letters, collects your money, tracks your affiliates and referrals, keeps everything organized, and saves you time (and headaches). In short, software enables you to grow and scale your business faster.

How Do You Get A Lot Of Clients?

Getting clients does not require traditional advertising, which is often like flushing money away. Instead, the most successful credit repair companies grow their client list by adding "Affiliates." Affiliates are often mortgage brokers, loan officers, realtors, auto dealers, insurance agents, CPAs and other financial professionals who have a daily flow of clients with credit issues. Put on a nice suit and get out and meet as many as you can. Offer them a nice commission for each "paid" client they refer to you. They will make extra money and will sell more loans, houses, and cars. Meanwhile, you'll have a nice, steady flow of clients: it's a win-win for everyone.

Credit Repair Works Because Of The Law

The Fair Credit Reporting Act gives you the right to dispute any item on a credit report. If that item can't be verified, it must be removed. This law is the basis of all credit repair. If you're starting a credit repair business it's important to understand the basic concepts of this law because this is how and why credit repair works.

The Fair Credit Reporting Act

The Fair Credit Reporting Act (FCRA) is a U.S. Federal Government legislation enacted to promote the accuracy, fairness, and privacy of consumer information contained in the files of consumer reporting agencies. It was intended to protect consumers from the willful and/or negligent inclusion of inaccurate information in their credit reports. To that end, the FCRA regulates the collection, dissemination, and use of consumer information, including consumer credit information. [1] Together with the Fair Debt Collection Practices Act (FDCPA), the FCRA forms the foundation of consumer rights law in the United States. It was originally passed in 1970.

Since your new business is made possible because of this law, it would be great for you to read through this summary of it. Enjoy!

A Summary Of Your Rights Under The Fair Credit Reporting Act

The Federal Fair Credit Reporting Act (FCRA) promotes the accuracy, fairness, and privacy of information in the files of consumer reporting agencies. There are many types of consumer reporting agencies, including credit bureaus and specialty agencies (such as agencies that sell information about check writing histories, medical records, and rental history records). Below is a summary of your major rights under the FCRA. For more information, including information about additional rights, go to www.ftc.gov/credit or write to:

Consumer Response Center, Room 130-A
Federal Trade Commission
600 Pennsylvania Ave. N.W.
Washington, D.C. 20580

You must be told if information in your file has been used against you. Anyone who uses a credit report or another type of consumer report to deny your application for credit, insurance, or employment — or to take another adverse action against you — must tell you and must give you the name, address, and phone number of the agency that provided the information.

You have the right to know what is in your file. You may request and obtain all the information about you in the files of a consumer reporting agency (your "file disclosure"). You will be required to provide proper identification, which may include your Social Security number. In many cases, the disclosure will be free.

You are entitled to a free file disclosure if:

- A person has taken adverse action against you because of information in your credit report

- You are the victim of identify theft and place a fraud alert in your file

- Your file contains inaccurate information as a result of fraud

- You are on public assistance

- You are unemployed but expect to apply for employment within 60 days

In addition, all consumers are entitled to one free disclosure every 12 months upon request from each nationwide credit bureau and from nationwide specialty consumer reporting agencies. See www.ftc.gov/credit for additional information.

You have the right to ask for your credit score. Credit scores are numerical summaries of your credit-worthiness based on information from credit bureaus. You may request a credit score from consumer reporting agencies that create scores or distribute scores used in residential real property loans, but you will have to pay for it. In some mortgage transactions you will receive credit score information for free from the mortgage lender.

You have the right to dispute incomplete or inaccurate information. If you identify information in your file that is incomplete or inaccurate, and report it to the consumer reporting agency, the agency must investigate (unless your dispute is deemed frivolous). See www.ftc.gov/credit for an explanation of dispute procedures.

Consumer reporting agencies must correct or delete inaccurate, incomplete, or unverifiable information, usually within 30 days. However, a consumer reporting agency may continue to report information it has verified as accurate.

Consumer reporting agencies may not report outdated negative information. In most cases, a consumer reporting agency may not report negative information that is more than seven years old or bankruptcies that are more than 10 years old.

Access to your file is limited. A consumer reporting agency may provide information about you only to people with a valid need — usually to consider an application with a creditor, insurer, employer, landlord, or other business. The FCRA specifies those with a valid need for access.

You must give your consent for reports to be provided to employers. A consumer reporting agency may not give out information about you to your employer, or a potential employer, without your written consent given to the employer. Written consent generally is not required in the trucking industry. For more information, visit to www.ftc.gov/credit.

You may limit "prescreened" offers of credit and insurance you get based on information in your credit report. You may opt-out with the nationwide credit bureaus at 1-888-5-OPTOUT (1-888-567-8688).

You may seek damages from violators. If a consumer reporting agency or, in some cases, a user of consumer reports or a furnisher of information to a consumer reporting agency, violates the FCRA you may be able to sue in state or federal court.

Identity theft victims and active duty military personnel have additional rights. For more information, visit www.ftc.gov/credit.

How To Have (And Maintain) Perfect Credit

Roughly one percent of the population has perfect credit, i.e., a FICO score of 850 (on a scale of 300 to 850).

Folks with such a high credit score all have these following traits in common:

- Between four and six revolving accounts (this means credit cards)

- At least one "installment" trade line (e.g., a mortgage or automobile loan) in good standing

- Several accounts around 20 years old with a long history of positive use (To get a score above 800, you need 10 years of positive account history)

- Around 30 years of credit use

- No late payments (or other serious account errors) for at least the past seven years

- Very few credit inquiries (no more than 1-3 in a six-month period)

- No derogatory notations; collections, bankruptcies, liens, judgments, etc.

- Debt levels on credit accounts of less than 35% of their overall credit limit

In other words, long but sparse use of several accounts without any payment issues along the way.

Now That You Know Their Simple Secret

Here's what *you* can do to follow their lead to improve your credit and keep it stellar for life:

See what everyone's saying about you:

Three major credit-reporting agencies are keeping tabs on what you do with your credit and finances. At least once a year (and a few months before entering into any major loan), review your credit reports from Equifax, Experian and TransUnion. You're entitled to one free copy from each bureau once a year (and more under certain circumstances).

Fix all typos and errors:

Since your credit record spans almost a decade of your borrowing activity, it makes sense that errors sometimes turn up. A recent study showed that 79% of all credit reports contain errors. Some common credit-reporting errors include out-of-date addresses, closed accounts being shown as open, credit lines not reported at the correct amount, and erroneous information.

Change your ways, immediately:

Self-inflicted credit wounds (such as a history of late payments, defaults, and irresponsible behavior in general) will fade from your record over time. Since the most recent behavior on your reports carry more weight than old news, vow that from this day forward you will be a financial upright citizen, and over time your score will grow.

Remember that a credit card is not cash. It represents money you do not have:

Even though you have been approved credit by a bank, a store, etc. (Visa, MasterCard, Sears, Kmart) to borrow thousands of dollars, you don't actually have thousands of dollars to spend, which leads nicely to the next rule...

Ignore anyone's rules on what should be an "acceptable" amount of debt:

Your debt-to-income ratio is the measure of how much debt you carry to how much money (after taxes) you have coming in. In the world of lending, it is acceptable to carry 25% of your income in debt. That ratio is still very high. You might want to consider trying to keep your debt (including car loans) to 15% or less of your after-tax income.

In summary:

Based on the above information, you can see that the trick to keeping your credit score high is to keep your spending under control, pay your bills on time, and don't apply for credit too often. Follow these rules and your credit score will begin to rise.

Dealing With Negative (But Correct) Information On Your Report

Despite popular belief, it is often possible to negotiate removal of negative items from your credit report. In some cases, you might not even have to pay the creditors the full amount owed*. The important thing is to be positive, be patient, and get in contact with your creditors to try to work out a deal.

If you've ignored (or never received) a creditor's bills or phone calls, or if you failed to keep up with payments, your bill may be turned over to a collection agency. Keep in mind that collection agencies are hired by the creditor and their only goal is to collect the money owed (or as much of it as they can) as quickly as possible. For their efforts, they are paid a percentage of what they collect.

If you feel that the amount in question is being billed in error, you have the right to ask for proof and verification of the charges. If the charges are indeed yours, it may be in your best interest to negotiate with the collection agency. You may be able to negotiate payment of the total sum (or even a partial amount) in return for a removal of their negative marks on your Credit History Report. You might be able to settle on paying a portion of your debt, or you might be able to work out a payment installment plan with them.

If you're a Credit Repair Cloud user, many of the creditor letters in the library can be used to negotiate with collection agencies for these situations. Whatever deal you make with them, be sure that you have it all in writing *prior* to paying them.

Collection agents can be very aggressive when it comes to collecting money. Remember that you have the right to ask a collection agency to stop contacting you, especially if you feel harassed. Many of the letters in our software (and in this book) will help to give you breathing room while working through your plan to reorganize your finances.

*See the letters in the Library section.

How Credit Bureaus Give Consumers The Run-Around

The dispute process can be unnecessarily long and frustrating. But why is that the case? Shouldn't credit bureaus want the most accurate information about consumers?

Unfortunately, the credit bureaus are often more concerned with profitability than accuracy. This is why credit repair companies have become so popular. The majority of consumer credit reports contain inaccuracies, inconsistencies, or outdated information; but consumers do not have the information or representation necessary to rectify them. Understanding the means by which credit bureaus gather information and investigate disputes is an important part of operating a successful credit repair company.

When a consumer sends in a dispute letter, it is first sent through the E-Oscar automated re-investigation system to filter out any duplicate or "frivolous" requests. The disputes are then electronically diluted into one of 26 two-digit codes. That code is then shared with the credit bureau to "investigate." The credit bureaus want to have a large quantity of data that can be sold to other organizations, so the accuracy of this data isn't as important to them as the quantity.

This is a very problematic system for several reasons. First, distilling a complicated issue down to a 2-digit code is an unacceptable oversimplification. This is especially true because over 40% of disputes are dumped in to a generic "catch all" category. Additionally, 70% of disputes employ nothing in the "comments" field to provide elaboration or explanation. It is impossible for these issues to be adequately explained in this situation. As a result, consumers are often frustrated because their disputes are not investigated based on the full nature of the issue, as outlined in their original dispute letter.

Another major problem with this system is the way that disputes are "investigated." When a consumer writes a dispute letter because information on their report is inaccurate, the bureau will investigate by consulting the same inaccurate information they have on file, thus "verifying" that the information is correct. This type of circular reasoning can be difficult for consumers to understand because false information is verified as correct based on the same false information.

In order to get around this exasperating and inefficient system consumers need to be empowered with the information necessary to submit a successful dispute. The best way to do this is to send back-up documentation for every dispute. This will force the bureaus to investigate your dispute beyond comparing it with their existing inaccurate information. Additionally it is crucial to hold the bureaus responsible by continually disputing requests on a strict timeline.

The Fair Credit Reporting Act (FCRA) gives bureaus 30 days to investigate each request. Consumers should follow up every 40 days to ensure that their disputes are not ignored. This is why it may be necessary to submit the same dispute multiple times. Finally, if all else fails, it is possible to pursue a lawsuit against the bureau for violating the FCRA by failing to properly investigate inaccurate information.

How To Negotiate Lower Credit Card Interest APR

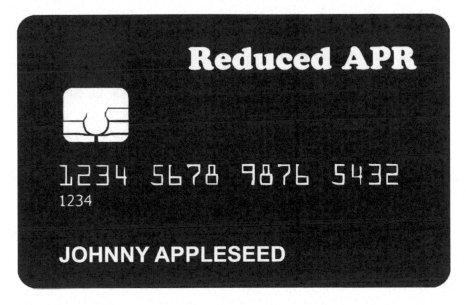

Credit card lenders usually charge anywhere from 0 to 20% in interest (APR), with the meanest banks charging as much as 30% (yikes)!

Most people do not realize that you can negotiate with your credit card company for a lower rate, especially if you've had any of your credit cards for a long time.

All you need to do is to call them up and insist on a lower rate. Shoot for 9-15%. You'll be surprised at how easy it is to save yourself a lot of money.

Here's how to do it:

1. Start with a credit card that you've had for a long time. One that you have never been late on with payments.

2. Look on the back of the card and dial the customer service number.

3. Start negotiating. Here's a sample script:

Sample script to reduce your APR:

You: (Upbeat and polite) "I just got an offer in the mail for a new credit card that has an introductory interest rate of only 6.9%! I don't really want to switch cards, because your service has been wonderful. But even though I've had your card for five years, I'm still paying a 19% rate on my balance. I'm going to have to transfer my balance unless you can lower the interest rate."

Them: (Over the sound of keyboard keys being tapped as your credit and payment history are being examined.) "Hmmm ... well, that is the standard rate... but let me see..."

You: "Of course, I understand that, but I can pay a lot less in interest if I transfer my balance. I really need you to reduce the rate to 9% or so."
Them: "Hold on while I check with my supervisor ... OK, how about 9.9%?"

You: "No problem." (Now pat yourself on the back for saving some bucks!)

This may not work as well if you're frequently late on your payments and over your head in debt. But it can't hurt to at least ask for an interest rate reduction. If you have a solid track record, handle your obligations and are generally polite, your lender should be willing to offer you a lower rate to keep from losing you to their competition.

Keep trying. If you don't get what you want the first time, try to get another customer service rep or a supervisor on the line. They still won't lower the APR? Mark your calendar to call them back in a few months.

Don't be angry. I have found that I am far more successful in all financial endeavors when being polite. These financial "gatekeepers" have angry people calling them all day long. Isn't it nice not to get yelled at for once? I've found that if you're nice and treat them with extra respect, they often return the favor and give you a little extra care.

7 Steps To Boost Your Credit Score

1. **Correct all inaccuracies on your credit report.**

   Go through your credit reports very carefully, looking for late payments, charge-offs, collections or other negative items that aren't yours.
   - Note accounts listed as "settled," "paid derogatory," "paid charge-off," or anything other than "current" or "paid as agreed" if you paid on time and in full.
   - Same goes for any accounts that were included in a bankruptcy but are still listed as unpaid, and negative items older than seven years (10 in the case of bankruptcy) that should have automatically fallen off your report.
   - *Warning: sometimes scores actually go down when bad items fall off your report - it's a quirk in the FICO credit-scoring software; you should still get rid of negative items*
   - Also make sure to remove any duplicate collection notices listed (for example, one from the creditor and one from the collections agency).

2. **Make sure that your proper credit lines are posted on your Credit Reports.**

   This seems bizarre, but often (in an effort to make you less desirable to their competitors) creditors will show you as having less available credit than you actually have. If you see this on your credit report, bring this to their attention. If you have bankruptcies that should be showing a zero balance…make sure they show a zero balance! Very often the creditor will not report a "bankruptcy charge-off" as a zero balance until it's been disputed.

3. **If you have any negative marks on your credit report, negotiate with the creditor/lender to remove them.**

   If you are a long-time customer and it's something simple like a one-time late payment, a creditor will often wipe it away to keep you as a loyal customer. If you have a serious negative mark (such as a long-overdue bill that has gone into collections), always negotiate a payment in exchange for removal of the negative item. Do not pay off a bill that has gone to collections unless the creditor agrees in writing that they will remove the derogatory item from your credit report. Also: never admit that the debt gone into collections is actually yours. Admission of debt can restart the statute of limitations and may enable the creditor to sue you. Admission also hurts your negotiating power. Simply say, "I'm calling about account number _____" instead of "I'm calling about my past due debt."

4. **Pay all credit cards and any revolving credit down to below 30% of the available credit line.**

The scoring system wants to make sure you aren't overextended, but at the same time, they want to see that you do indeed use your credit. 30% of the available credit line seems to be the magic "balance vs. credit line" ratio to have. For example; if you have a credit card with a $10,000 credit line, make sure that your balance is never more than $3000 (even if you pay your account off in full each month). You can also try asking your long-time creditors if they will raise your credit line without checking your FICO score or your credit report. Tell them that you're shopping for a house and you can't afford to have any hits on your credit report.

5. **Do not close your old credit card accounts.**

Old established accounts show your history and testify to your stability and good payment habits. Cut up the cards if you don't want to use them, but keep the accounts open.

6. **Avoid applying for new credit.**

Each time you apply for new credit, your credit report gets dinged with an inquiry. New credit cards will not help your credit score and a credit account less than one year old may hurt your credit score. Use your cards and credit as little as possible until the next credit scoring.

7. **Have at least three revolving credit lines and one active (or paid) installment loan listed on your Credit Report.**

The scoring system wants to see that you maintain a variety of credit accounts. It also wants to see that you have at least three revolving credit lines - so make sure you do. If you have poor credit and are not approved for a typical credit card, you might want to set up a "secured credit card" account. This means that you will have to make a deposit that is equal to or more than your limit, which guarantees the bank that you will repay the loan. It's an excellent way to establish credit. Installment loans, car loans, furniture/appliance loans, or mortgages (best of all) all qualify.

Throughout this process, always remember:

It takes up to 30 Days for any of these things to get reported and sometimes another 30 days to reflect on your credit history reports. It feels like a slow process, but hang in there because it does work.

This tedious process can be made much simpler with software: especially if you're running credit repair as a business. Credit Repair Cloud stores your user information to auto populate the disputes, saving you many long hours of letter writing.

Credit Dispute Overview

Basic Steps To Repairing Credit For Clients

When you first start a credit repair company, it can be difficult to filter through all the available information and determine where to begin with a new client. While each client is different and your approach to each will vary, the basic process outlined here will give you a general framework for moving forward.

Step 1: Acquire and analyze your client's credit reports.
Get a copy of your client's credit report from each credit bureau. Once you have copies of each, dissect them to find inaccuracies, redundancies, or unverifiable information that can be disputed. Sit down with your client to determine a course of action. Make sure to educate your client on what they can expect and what you will need from them (i.e., updating you on responses from bureaus in a timely manner).

Step 2: Draft dispute letters.
Create your dispute letters. Make sure to list each item that you are disputing and the reason(s) why. Include all supporting documentation (payment receipts, etc.) and copies of your client's identification documents. Don't procrastinate or wait to receive all credit reports. Remember to duplicate all correspondence for your client's file. This will be essential if a lawsuit becomes necessary.

Step 3: Send and track dispute letters.
Send the letters as soon as possible. We highly recommend sending them via certified mail with return receipt so you know exactly when the bureau receives your dispute. The Fair Credit Reporting Act (FCRA) gives the bureau 30 days to investigate a claim. Set a reminder on your calendar so you know when to follow up with the client to see if he/she has received a response, so you can act on it ASAP.

Step 4: Collect responses from clients.
The credit bureau will respond to your client directly via mail. The response will indicate either that the dispute was confirmed and modified/removed from the credit report or that the item was confirmed and will remain. If you are using Credit Repair Cloud, have the client take a photo of the response with their smartphone and upload it to your

portal. This is typically the most effective way to collect responses. If you do not use the software, you can ask clients to mail you copies, or scan and email/fax them to you.

Step 5: Follow up. Be persistent!
If the bureau has not removed the item from your client's credit report, send a follow-up letter reiterating the dispute and the reasoning behind it. You may have to dispute the same item several times. Remember to reword the letter so that the bureau's computer systems don't reject it as "frivolous." Check items that were removed off of the action plan you made in Step 1. This will show clients that your interventions are worthwhile.

Patience and persistence are key to successful credit repair. At the beginning of the process, manage your clients' expectations. Tell them that it may take several tries and could take months. That way, they will understand responses and will handle negative responses from the bureaus better.

How To Read The Client's Credit Reports

This is the most important step when you are first working with a client.

1. Take time to carefully review the credit reports with your client
2. Circle the items you wish to dispute
3. Choose which items to dispute first

Always start with the easiest disputes that contain the most blatant errors. This will help you to wow your clients with fast results.

Remember: "most" credit reports contain errors. It's your job to find them.

A recent study found that 79% of credit reports contain errors that lower the score. As a credit repair professional this is great news to you because it means that most reports can be improved immediately by simply disputing these errors.

Common errors include false delinquencies, public records, judgments, and credit accounts that did not belong to the consumer. Sometimes these errors are the work of sloppy data entry and sometimes they're due to identity theft. It is important to examine the credit reports carefully and make every effort to correct, update, or delete ALL unfavorable and incorrect information.

A credit report is filled with following sections:

1. **Identification Information:** Name, date of birth, and social security number. These are used for identification. Sometimes, the report also includes your employment information, current and past addresses, and spouse's name and date of birth.

2. **Public Record Information:** Data from federal, state or county court records, bankruptcies, liens or judgments and other types of claims. This includes the date filed, court case number, amount, status, and date settled.

3. **Collection Agency Information:** A collection is an account that has been turned over to a collection agency by one of your creditors because you have not paid the account as agreed. Listed here are: collector's name, originating creditor/client, original amount, balance due, and account number.

4. **Credit Information:** This section makes up the bulk of the report. It will include Mortgage, Installment, Revolving, Other, Open and Closed Accounts. It will also list Accounts in Good Standing, Accounts Currently Past due, and Negative Account History.

The credit Information section is laid out as follows:

- Merchant/Creditor name
- Subscriber number
- Account number
- Date opened
- Date closed
- Current Balance
- Highest credit limit
- Highest amount of credit used, and
- Your Repayment History

Your Repayment History is shown as a string of numbers showing your payment history. Listed with each credit account are the account's status and history. They are generally marked as follows:

- Current Account
- Account Open or Closed in Good Standing
- Closed Account
- Credit Account Closed
- Paid Account
- Closed Account or Zero Balance
- Credit Account Reinstated
- Previously Closed Account Now Available for use
- Foreclosure
- Collateral sold to collect Defaulted Mortgage
- Collection Account
- Credit Account Assigned to Collection Agency

5. **Inquiries that display to others:** All authorized and legitimate requests from companies, creditors, employers, etc., to see your credit history are listed.

6. **Inquiries that DO NOT display to others:** These inquiries are displayed only to you and are not considered when tabulating your

credit score. Examples of these kinds of inquiries are: pre-approved offers of credit, insurance, or periodic account reviews by an existing creditor.

7. **Consumer Statement:** If for some reason you cannot prove that a negative item is an error or if you are having a disagreement with a certain creditor, you have the right to tell your side of the story in 100 words or fewer. This statement will be added to your report.

What to look for:

- *Incorrect or incomplete personal information:* Pay attention to name, address, phone number, social security number or birth date, as well as missing, incorrect, or outdated employment information. Also check for incorrect marital status (for example, a former spouse listed as current spouse).

- *Outdated items past their statute of limitations:*
  - Bankruptcies older than 10 years
  - Lawsuits or judgments, tax liens, criminal records or delinquent accounts more than 7 years old
  - Inquiries over 2 years old

- *Account details and status:* Make sure your accounts, credit limits and balances are listed correctly; If YOU closed an account, it should say "Account closed by consumer." If a credit limit is not posted accurately, this can lower the score.

- *Accounts you don't recognize:* If you see a credit account you don't recall opening or charges you haven't made, this is something to be taken very seriously, as it may be an indication of Identity Theft.

- *Delinquencies you didn't cause*

- *Duplicate accounts:* Once in a while, an error may be made that may cause a legitimate credit account to be listed more than one time on your report. These are fairly easy to catch, as they will appear identical. The problem is that they will contribute to the total debt owed and number of active accounts.

- *Inquiries you don't recognize or that are over 2 years old:* Inquiries must be authorized. They also should disappear from the report after two years.

Most negative information (except for public records/court filings) should fall off a credit report after <u>seven years</u>, giving you a fresh start. If you see late payments, delinquent accounts, or collection activity after the time they should have been removed you should request their removal.

If you suspect identity theft or fraud on one of your reports, contact that credit bureau IMMEDIATELY. Explain the situation and ask them to place a fraud alert on your file. Also report the fraud to the police.

Online credit reports never show full account numbers, and that's good, because it protects the consumers. They only show a partial number with XXX's. So those partial numbers with XXX's are exactly what should be on the dispute letters that you send.

The Basics Of The Dispute Process

The best method to remove inaccurate or unverifiable information from a credit report is with the dispute process. Under the Federal Fair Credit Reporting Act (FCRA), individuals are given the right to dispute any items on their credit reports that are incomplete, inaccurate, unverifiable or untimely. If those items cannot be verified they must be removed. This is the basis of all credit repair.

This practice can be lengthy and frustrating, but ultimately successful in improving your credit.

Always Be Transparent With Your Clients

Before you begin, make sure your client is involved in determining what you're disputing for them and why. The dispute letters are coming from the client, so this is a time for total transparency. Plus, disputing something without the client's awareness can get you into serious legal trouble.

In Credit Repair Cloud, we have a feature that you can enable called "Client's Choice." This gives the client the responsibility of choosing what to dispute and why, protecting your business from any misunderstandings.

Sending "Rounds" Of Dispute Letters

Letters are sent in "Rounds."

- **A Round 1 letter** is sent to the Credit Bureaus. It can be about *multiple* items (try to keep it to five or less per bureau, per month).

- **A Round 2** (or higher) **letter** is sent to a specific bureau or a creditor. It is always about *one* item.

Start by sending letters to the appropriate bureau listing the items you are challenging and the reason for dispute. Make two copies of every letter you send so you can include one in your filing system for your records. Some letters you may want to send via certified mail with return receipt.

Common Dispute Reasons

There are several reasons to dispute an item on your credit report. The most common are:

- Items on the account are misleading or questionable
- The account is not yours
- Balances are inaccurate
- You have not received a notice of late payment
- Trade line amounts are incorrect
- Account numbers are listed incorrectly
- Accounts are unverifiable
- The original creditor is listed incorrectly
- The charge-off date or amount is listed incorrectly
- The date of last activity is inaccurate
- The credit limit is listed incorrectly
- The account status is inaccurate

Creating Your Action Plan

In this chapter, we will explore how to go through the dispute process in detail. The steps to be discussed are:

1. Study the Fair Credit Reporting Act (FCRA) to understand what types of items can be disputed.

2. Review your credit report for any inaccuracies that can be disputed.

3. Decide which dispute technique you will use: debt settlement, direct dispute, or suing the credit bureaus.

4. Create a system to keep track of ongoing correspondence with the credit bureaus.

5. Refer to the six-step dispute letter plan and begin sending dispute letters to credit bureaus. Make sure to send all letters via certified mail with return receipts.

Step 1: Understanding The Fair Credit Reporting Act (FCRA)

The Fair Credit Reporting Act (FCRA) is a federal law that regulates the collection, circulation, and use of consumer credit information. Under the FCRA, the credit bureaus have three primary responsibilities to consumers regarding credit reports:

- Credit bureaus must provide consumers with all information on their individual credit reports and must make all reasonable efforts to investigate any disputed items

- If any items are removed as the result of a dispute, they may not be re-added without notifying the consumer

- Bureaus may not retain information for an excessive amount of time. This is typically considered 7 years for late payments and tax liens and 10 years for bankruptcies.

Step 2: Reviewing A Credit Report - What To Look For

The first step in the dispute process is to review with your client a copy of their credit report.

Start with the easy part: personal information. Review the name, address, social security number, employment history, etc., for any inaccuracies. This is very important because inaccurate personal information is often a sign of identity theft.

Once you have done this, get started with your account and balance inquiries. When reviewing a credit report, there are three primary types of discrepancies to look out for:

1. Trade Line Inaccuracies
   - Late payments
   - Tax liens

- Repossession, when it should be listed as "involuntarily surrendered"
- Judgments
- Collections
- Debt consolidation
- Charge-offs
- Bankruptcies that were not dismissed or withdrawn
- Delinquencies older than 7 years
- Bankruptcies or court recorded events older than 10 years

2. Account/Inquiry Discrepancies
   - Unauthorized users
   - Individuals listed as deceased
   - Inaccurate last day of activity
   - Inaccurate accounts as a result of divorce
   - Attempts to foreclose
   - Inaccurate negative cosigned accounts
   - Unauthorized inquiries
   - Consumer credit counseling loan indications

3. Balance Discrepancies
   - Paid accounts still showing debt
   - Incorrect balances or credit limits
   - Missing credit lines
   - Signs of identity theft
   - Duplicate collection items
   - Closed accounts that are listed as open
   - Accounts that you have closed but are listed as "closed by creditor" and vice versa

Go through your report with a highlighter and mark any items that are inaccurate, outdated, or misleading. Then make a list of the items you would like to dispute. Start with the easier ones, such as outdated accounts, inaccurate late payments, settled accounts, and authorized user accounts. It is more difficult to dispute inaccurate bankruptcies, foreclosures and repossessions, unpaid tax liens, and child support.

Step 3: Decide On Your Dispute Technique

There are three primary methods by which to dispute the items you have identified on your credit report:

Account Settlement

The easiest method for quickly improving your report is to settle with your creditors. This method will cost you, but may result in the items on your report being completely removed. So if the item on your report is accurate and you have the money to pay it off, this may be your best option. Whatever deal you make with them, be sure that you have it all in writing prior to paying this settlement.

Basic Dispute Process

The basic dispute process, outlined in this chapter, is the most common way to dispute inaccuracies on a credit report. This process involves reviewing the reports and writing letters to credit bureaus to have inaccuracies removed. This can be a frustrating process, as responses from the bureaus are often slow or nonexistent (which can sometimes work in your favor, as discussed below).

Suing the Credit Bureau

If you have attempted to dispute one or more items on your report and have not received a response from the credit bureau within 30 days, or if the bureau refused to investigate, you may be able to initiate a lawsuit. This will likely yield a successful result, as the bureau would be in violation of the Fair Credit Reporting Act (FCRA). If you believe you have a basis for a lawsuit, we recommend contacting a credit attorney to discuss the next steps. A credit attorney is an important element. They will often work on a contingency basis with no cost to you or your client.

Step 4: Create A System To Track Correspondence With Credit Bureaus

Throughout the dispute process it is crucial to log every piece of correspondence sent to or received from the credit bureaus. If the bureaus fail to adequately investigate your dispute, documentation of your ongoing attempts to contact them will be necessary for a lawsuit or other future legal action. All correspondence sent to the bureaus should be sent via certified mail with return receipt so you can keep track of when each was sent and received. This is important to have for proof for legal action, as well as for your own follow-up plan.

We recommend creating a filing system with folders for each of the three bureaus so this information will always be easily at your fingertips. It is helpful to create a tracking form to keep in the folder as a sort of table of contents for the folder's contents. The form should include the document's tracking number, date sent, number of disputed items, and the date you plan to follow up.

Pro Tips For Writing Dispute Letters

Challenge everything you feel is inaccurate, but never dispute more than five items per bureau per month. The largest and most successful credit repair companies only dispute two to three items per month. If you dispute more than that, your letters will be flagged as frivolous and rejected — and this is difficult to overcome. Follow these steps for your best chance of successfully getting negative items removed:

- Dispute the obvious errors (easiest items) first

- Don't give up: if the bureaus fail to address your requests, they are in violation of the law

- Inaccuracies should be disputed time and time again until they are removed: don't take no for an answer

- Set calendar notifications to remind yourself to follow up 30-40 days after the bureau received your request so you do not fall behind *(If you use Credit Repair Cloud, reminders are built in)*

- If the bureau responds that you should follow up with the creditor, respond that you have already done so and the creditor directed you back to them.

Once the credit bureau receives your request, they have 30 days to respond that either the item was revised/deleted or it has been verified and will not be changed. Remember, it is your right to demand proof of how the debt was verified.

Sending Dispute Letters In Rounds

Letter #1 (Round 1)

Your initial letter should include the following information and documentation. Be polite and professional in this initial letter in order to elicit the most favorable response.

- Your credit report number (unless it's an online credit report as those have no numbers)

- A copy of your credit report with the disputed items highlighted or circled (optional)

- The item you are disputing

- The reason for the dispute (such as: "This is not my account")

- The instructions for the bureau (such as: "Please remove this inaccurate information from my Credit report")

- Any dooumentation that can prove your dispute (receipts of pay-off, confirmation emails, etc.)

- A signature

For a Round 1 letter, always include:

- A copy of your client's driver's license or government issued photo ID to prove identity (required)

- A copy of a utility bill, insurance bill, or bank statement as proof of address (required)

As a rule of thumb, the letters are always as simple as possible. There's no need for threats, anger, or legalese. There's also no need to worry about it looking like a form letter. All that matters is that you state simple concise facts.

*For sample dispute letters see the chapter of Sample Dispute Letters.

Pursuing A Lawsuit

If you have attempted to dispute one or more items on your report and have not received a response from the credit bureau within 30 days, or if the bureau refused to investigate, you may be able to initiate a lawsuit. This will likely yield a successful result, as the bureau would be in violation of the Fair Credit Reporting Act (FCRA).

If you believe you have a basis for a lawsuit, we recommend contacting a credit attorney to discuss the next steps. A credit attorney is an important element. They will often work on a contingency basis <u>with no cost to you or your client unless they win a settlement for your client.</u>

Using Factual Dispute Methodology

When you're starting a credit repair business, you have a choice of what kind of company you're going to build. A good and honest company slowly builds a fantastic business with happy clients and a steady stream of referrals. This business grows organically and pragmatically on a foundation that will last, whereas a company that operates in the grey might make a quick buck for a moment, but will disappear just as quickly. The key to success is a solid foundation.

The reason that credit repair companies have gotten a bad rap for being unethical or dishonest is largely due to the way that some credit repair companies have chosen to operate. Some of these unethical companies do credit repair by simply asserting that all negative items on their clients credit reports are due to identity theft and crossing their fingers that some will be removed. This is not credit repair — it is fraud.

Many credit repair companies who operate in the grey will dispute items without their client knowing what is being disputed and why. Not only is this unethical, but it can have serious legal consequences.

Yes, the Fair Credit Reporting Act (FCRA) gives a consumer the right to dispute anything on a credit report. And yes, accurate items can be challenged and removed if they cannot be verified, but it all must be done in a correct, smart, and legal way.

True credit repair requires skill, experience, and patience. Ethical credit repair professionals go through their clients' credit reports together with their clients to find information that is false, unverifiable, or incomplete. They then contact the bureaus to have it modified or removed. We call this strategy the **Factual Dispute Methodology**.

The Factual Dispute Methodology is an important distinction for credit repair companies who seek to help people restore their standing by referencing the Fair Credit Reporting Act (FCRA) to dispute inaccurate information. Nearly 80 percent of all credit reports in the US have inaccuracies that need to be modified. Your role is to find these inaccuracies and create a plan of action to dispute them.

There are several types of negative items you will find on a consumer's credit report, including inquiries, late payments, collections, bankruptcies, foreclosures, repossessions, judgments, and charge-offs. When examining a credit report, the first step is to determine whether each piece of information adheres to the following standards:

Is it accurate?

Check that all account numbers, dates, account status, account types, and other information is correct based on the consumer's personal records. Check that the credit reports you have accessed from all three bureaus contain the same exact information.

Is it complete?

There should be no missing dates, account numbers, balances, or other information. This is one of the most common errors you will find on a credit report.

Is it verifiable?

Creditors are required by law to have back up documentation for everything that is listed on a credit report. If the information does not exist then the item should be removed completely. Are the records murky? Is there no signature from the client?

Once you have marked up the credit report with the items that are inaccurate, incomplete, or unverifiable, prioritize those that you will dispute first.

Many people choose to start with the easiest or most glaringly non-compliant items, then move on to the more difficult ones. This is often the best route because your clients will see results faster.

Others prioritize based on how much the item affects the consumer's total credit score. For this strategy, it is helpful to know how scores are created. Credit scores are reported based on the following approximate formula:

- 35% payment history
- 30% amounts owed
- 15% length of credit history
- 10% inquiries/recent credit decisions
- 10% types of credit used

Understanding this information, it would make sense to tackle the non-compliant items related to payment history and amounts owed first before moving on to other discrepancies.

Yes, it takes some time to go through the report this way; but the good news is that you only need to do this once for each client. If you're using the Credit Repair Cloud software, you will tag all the items you wish to dispute when you import the credit report. This "tagging" maps out your course for the lifecycle of this client. If you've done this correctly at the start, then each month that follows should take you less than 5 minutes of work, clicking to dispute a few more items on your list (these are the "Round 1" letters) — or replying to the response letters that were sent to your client (these are "Round 2" and higher).

Throughout the client's lifecycle, don't forget that it's equally important to educate them to better manage their credit. Explain what they can do to help to speed up the credit repair process, to pay down balances, to stop maxing out their cards, and to stop applying for credit. Help them change their bad credit habits so they can maintain their good credit long after your work is done. Those extra touches are what will build your referrals. We have many tools and resources in the Credit Repair Cloud client portal to help you with this, but it's up to you to go the extra mile and be awesome for your clients. This will grow your business much faster than trickery.

Understanding and adhering to the Factual Dispute Methodology, and involving and educating your clients are key parts to operating an ethical, trustworthy credit repair business. It is up to all of us to adhere to high legal and ethical standards so we can change the conversation around credit repair to a more positive one.

Remember: you have an opportunity to truly help people. Approaching it that way will make a difference in your community — and it's good karma.

Starting Your Dispute

Make certain that all information is current and accurate, including the Personal Identification information (address, social security, etc...). If you find an error (for example, a loan that you have PAID OFF is still listed as outstanding), tell the Credit Bureau (in writing) EXACTLY what the mistake is, and explain the way that the information SHOULD be listed. For example, "My Loan to Bank of Fred is NOT outstanding. It was paid in full on 02/14/2009." Send photocopies along with all the necessary information to back up your claim.

After you have done this, send it to the credit bureau by "CERTIFIED MAIL." When the credit bureau receives your report and the information in question, they are required to investigate and ADVISE YOU of the results of their investigation. They must do this free of charge.

Anytime that you are denied credit, you have the right to know why. If a store denies you credit, they send you a letter with an explanation. If the store based their decision on your credit history, they must provide you with the name and address of the agency that reported it.

If for some reason you cannot prove that a negative item is in error or if you are having a disagreement with a certain creditor, you have the right to tell your side of the story in 100 words or less. This statement will be ADDED to your report.

When correcting items on your credit report, you have the right to demand that the credit bureau send corrected copies of your report to all creditors who have received the incorrect reports for the past six months.

Note: Credit bureaus will not do this automatically! They will only do it if you ask. So make sure you ask. It's your right!

Choosing A Dispute Letter

Which Dispute Letter Should I Send?

Which letter to send depends about what you are disputing, why (and which round you're on).

If you're a Credit Repair Cloud user, you have access to over 100 letters to cover you for just about any situation, but you will probably only use a handful of them. You'll find a few favorites that you use again and again.

Yes, but which letter do I use right now?

Just starting? Here's a basic rule of thumb to follow; no matter what you're disputing, all disputes start with the very same "Default Round 1 Letter." This letter is sent to credit bureaus, it is intentionally simple and should not be used to dispute more than 5 items. In fact, the most successful companies only dispute 2-3 items per month per bureau. In this letter you'll simply explain which account has the error, the reason for the dispute and instructions for the bureau. If you're a Credit Repair Cloud user, you create this letter in Wizard 3 with just a few clicks.

Your client should drive the decisions

Really? Yes, your client should tell you what they are disputing and why. For that reason you'll always start with an interview with the client to review the reports and come up with your game strategy.

Choosing The Right Dispute Letter

There are over 100 letters in the Credit Repair Cloud library, separated into 4 categories; Default letters, Credit Bureau letters, Creditor letters, Collections letters, Misc. letters, and you can also add your own custom letters. Here's a breakdown of each category:

Default letters

These 2 simple letters are the defaults for the Wizard.

- Request Credit Report (Default for Wizard 1)
- Dispute Credit Report Items (Default for Wizard 3-Round 1)

"Request Credit Report" requests a credit report directly from the bureaus by paper mail, but you probably won't be needing that one because (a) those reports won't have scores, and two, they can't be imported into software. Instead, you'll have your client order online reports and scores instantly from an online service like IdentityIQ, SmartCredit, MyFreeScoreNow, IdentityClub and PrivacyGuard. These providers come and go, so you'll find a complete and current list in your Credit Repair Cloud under MY COMPANY>CREDIT MONITORING SERVICE.

"Dispute Credit Report Items (Default for Wizard 3-Round 1)" is **the most important letter in our software and it's the one you will use most often**. It is the "Default Round 1 letter." All disputes start with this letter. It's a very simple letter with no legalese. If you're not a Credit Repair Cloud user, there's a copy of that letter in this book.

All other letter categories listed below are for round 2 or higher. They are for sending directly to the bureau, a creditor or a collections agent. Once you've sent your round 1 letter and you've received a response from the bureau, that is when you're going to reply with one of these Round 2 (or higher) letters below.

Credit Bureau Letters

These letters are sent directly to the credit bureaus as a reply to their response letter. These letters are generally about just one dispute item.
- Dispute Credit Report Items (Round 1 Alternate)
- Dispute Credit Report Items (Round 1 Alternate 2)
  Dispute Credit Report Items (Round 1 Alternate 3)
- Request Removal after Bureau Investigation
- Request Removal after Creditor Verification
- Dispute Follow-up after no response for 30 days
- Dispute Follow-up after no response for 60 days
- Dispute After Investigation: "The Prove it" Letter
- Request to Describe Investigation Procedures
- Demand to Comply with Investigation Request
- Dispute Accounts That Should Be Included In BK
- Validate Debt
- Victim of Identity Theft
- Report Identity Theft
  Report Identity Theft (Alternate)
- Request to Merge Spouse's Credit History
- Request to Add Additional Credit Information
- Credit Inquiry Removal Request
  100 Word Consumer Statement
- Frivolous Dispute Response
  Frivolous Dispute Response (Alternate)
- Reply to Accusation of Credit Repair
- Intention to File FTC Complaint - After 30 Days
- Intention to File FTC Complaint - After 30 Days (Alternate)
- Intention to File FTC Complaint - After 60 Days
- Intent To File Lawsuit for FCRA Violation

Creditor Letters

These "Round 2" (and higher) letters are sent directly to the creditor and they are generally about just one dispute item.

- Dispute Credit Card Bill
- Error on Credit Card Bill
- Request Removal of Incorrect Info
- Request Removal of Incorrect Info (Alternate)
- Request Direct Negotiation with Creditor
- Pay for Delete (Offer Payment if Negative is Removed)
- Pay For Delete (Alternate)
- Pay For Delete (Alternate 2)
- Debt Settlement Offer
- Debt Settlement Offer (Alternate)
- Debt Settlement Offer (Alternate 2)
- Debt Settlement Offer (Alternate 3)
- Debt Settlement Offer to Dismiss Court Judgment
- Unilateral Release of Claims (Include with Settlement Offer Before Payment)
- Cashed Check Constitutes Payment in Full
- Request Smaller Payments (Short Term)
- Request Smaller Payments (Long Term)
- Request No Payments (Short Term)
- Request No Payments (Long Term)
- Remove Hard Inquiry
- Remove Hard Inquiry (Alternate)
- Dispute Item
- Dispute Item (Alternate)
- Validation of Debt (Simple)
- Validation of Debt (Alternate)
- Validation of Debt (Alternate 2)
- Validation of Debt (Alternate 3)
- Validation of Debt (Alternate 4)
- Validation of Debt (After Dispute to Bureau)
- Validation of Debt (Estoppel by Silence)
- Validation of Debt (Admission by Silence)
- Validation of Debt with Creditor Disclosure Statement

- Validation of Debt with Creditor Disclosure Statement (Alternate)
- Validation of Debt with Creditor Disclosure Statement) (Alternate 2)
- Validation of Medical Debt (HIPAA Request)
- Goodwill Letter sent to Original Creditor
- Goodwill Adjustment Letter
- Inform a Creditor that you have filed for Bankruptcy
- Inform Creditor of Bankruptcy
- Reaffirming Debt After Bankruptcy
- Agreement Offer Settlement to Dismiss Judgment
- Agreement to Dismiss Court Judgment
- Judgment Proof Letter
- Judgment Proof Letter (Alternate)
- Request Original Creditor to Take Back Debt from Collection Agency
- Warning of VOD refusal and FDCPA violations
- Warning Violation for Expired Debt Collection
- Warning Violation for Expired Debt Collection (Alternate)
- Warning of Expired Statute of Limitations
- Pay For Delete (Alternate 3)

Collections Letters

These "Round 2" (and higher) letters are sent directly to the collections agent and they are generally about just one dispute item.
- Basic Dispute for Collections
- Debt Settlement Offer (Alternate)
- Dispute Collections
- Temporarily Stop Collections
- Pay for Delete (Offer Payment if Negative is Removed)
- Pay For Delete (Alternate)
- Pay For Delete (Alternate 2)
- Pay For Delete (Alternate 3)
- Debt Settlement Offer
- Debt Settlement Offer (Alternate 2)
- Debt Settlement Offer (Alternate 3)
- Debt Settlement Offer to Dismiss Court Judgment
- Unilateral Release of Claims (Include with Offer Before Payment)
- Validation of Debt (Simple)

- Validation of Debt (Alternate)
- Validation of Debt (Alternate 2)
- Validation of Debt (Alternate 3)
- Validation of Debt (Alternate 4)
- Validation of Debt (After Dispute to Bureau)
- Validation of Debt (Estoppel by Silence)
- Validation of Debt (Admission by Silence)
- Validation of Debt with Creditor Disclosure Statement
- Validation of Debt with Creditor Disclosure Statement (Alternate)
- Validation of Debt with Creditor Disclosure Statement) (Alternate 2)
- Validation of Medical Debt (HIPAA Request)
- Judgment Proof Letter
- Judgment Proof Letter (Alternate)
- Inform a Creditor that you have filed for Bankruptcy
- Inform Creditor of Bankruptcy
- Cease and Desist
- Cease and Desist (Alternate)
- Cease and Desist (Alternate 2)
- Complaint about Harassment
- Warning of VOD refusal and FDCPA violations
- Warning Violation for Expired Debt Collection
- Warning Violation for Expired Debt Collection (Alternate)
- Warning of Expired Statute of Limitations

Misc. Letters

These letters are for special circumstances. Again, the titles are self sufficient. Use the one that best fits your situation.

- ChexSystem (Request Report)
- ChexSystems (Request Investigation)
- Request for Loan Modification
- Letter Of Hardship For Loan Modification
- Letter Of Hardship For Loan Modification (Alternate)
- Letter Of Hardship For Loan Modification (Alternate 2)
- Letter to Dismiss Court Judgment

But Which Letter Do I Send For Round 2 And Higher?

Which letter to send for Round 2 (and higher) depends on the client's particular situation and on how the credit bureaus respond to the Round 1 letter. Every client's situation is different, so there is no catch all answer for this other than this comes with experience, logic and reading through your library of letters to find one that is appropriate for the situation. However, we've made this decision very easy in Credit Repair Cloud with our new "Letter Finder" feature. It asks a few questions and then suggests the perfect letter for you.

Examples

If you're a Credit Repair Cloud user, there are over 130 letters and they can cover any situation. But if you look closely, there are many versions for each common situation. Read through the letters, mark a few as favorites (with the heart icon) and choose the letter that best describes your client's circumstances and the error they are reporting. Here are some common examples:

If your client has an account listed that's not theirs

For this you will probably send a round 2 letter demanding validation or proof of verification to the bureau, and possibly later on, to the creditor. You also might like to send "The Prove it" Letter. With a validation or verification letter, you are asking for proof that the client signed up and agreed to these charges, acceptable verification would be a signature, a verbal recording, etc. In many cases, that proof does not really exist, so the item gets removed. In Credit Repair Cloud there are more than 20 verification and validation letters. Read through them all to decide which one best fits this client's situation.

If the bureau, creditor or collections refuse to validate the debt

You might want to send Warning of VOD refusal and FDCPA violation —
or Warning Violation for Expired Debt Collection.

If your client was a victim of identity theft

Use the credit bureau letter that called "Victim of Identity Theft"

If you're not a Credit Repair Cloud user, see the Sample Letters chapter
for an assortment of sample dispute letters..

Sample Basic Round 1 Dispute Letter

A credit dispute always starts with a Round 1 letter to a credit bureau. It never goes to a creditor. Here is a sample Round 1 letter with sample dispute items. Use the ones you need (up to five) and delete the rest.

Your Name
Your Address
City, State Zip
Your Date of Birth:
Last 4 of Social Security:

Credit Bureau Name
Credit Bureau Address
City, State Zip

Today's Date

Re: Letter to Remove Inaccurate Credit Information – Credit Report
#_____

To Whom It May Concern:

I received a copy of my credit report and found the following item(s) to have errors.

Incorrect Personal Information:
XXXXXXXXXXXXXXXX

Correct Personal Information:
XXXXXXXXXXXXX

The following accounts below are not mine:
Creditor's Name
Account Number
Explanation:

The account status is incorrect for the following accounts:

Creditor's Name
Account Number
Correct Status:

The following information is outdated. I would like it removed from my credit history report:

Creditor's Name
Account Number
Date of Last Activity

The following inquiries are more than two years old and I would like them removed:
Creditor's Name
Date of Inquiry

These inquiries below were not authorized:
Creditor's Name
Date of Inquiry
Explanation

The following accounts were closed by me and should state that:
Creditor's Name
Account Number

Other information I would like changed:
Explanation

By the provisions of the Fair Credit Reporting Act, I demand that these items be investigated and removed from my report.
It is my understanding that you will recheck these items with the creditor who has posted them. Please remove any information that the creditor cannot verify.

I understand that under 15 U.S.C. Sec. 1681i(a), you must complete this reinvestigation within 30 days of receipt of this letter. Please send an updated copy of my credit report to the above address. According to the act, there shall be no charge for this updated report.

I also request that you please send notices of corrections to anyone who received my credit report in the past six months.

Thank you for your time and help in this matter.

Sincerely,

_____

[Signature]

Include a copy of your government issued Photo ID (like your drivers license or passport) and proof of address (like a utility or insurance bill). Also include copies (not originals) of any paperwork you may have that validates your claims.

Round 2 (And Higher)

Many people ask us about what happens after you send a Round 1 letter:

- How do I respond to the bureaus?
- How do I update items?
- What about other rounds?

These are all great questions.

The simple answer is that for each dispute letter you send, your client will get a letter back (that they need to share with you). That letter will always explain what was removed (or not removed) and why.

After that, there are 2 ways to proceed:

SCENARIO 1 (item was removed): The new report is imported and the item has been deleted (or, you receive a letter that says the item was deleted, and you go to the "Dispute Items" page in that client's account in Credit Repair Cloud and change the status to deleted). Once the item's status has changed to "Deleted," your client is sent a notification from Credit Repair Cloud — and you look like a hero!

SCENARIO 2 (item was not removed): If the letter comes back and says that the item was validated, you can challenge that validation, with a "Round 2" Letter (or higher).

What's a Round 2 (or higher) letter?

A "Round 2" letter (or higher) disputes one (1) item and can be sent to the credit bureau or to the creditor/furnisher who is reporting the item.

Which Letter to choose?

We recommend that you read through all the Credit Repair Cloud Library Letters. You can mark your favorites by clicking the heart icon. Every situation is different, so get to know the letters and develop a feel for which situation warrants each letter.

Creating A Round 2 (Or Higher) Letter

If you started this client by importing their report, you don't need to import it again. Since the Round 2 letter is a follow-up to what you disputed in Round 1, just go directly to Wizard 3:

A) Choose Radio Button #2 for Round 2 and then choose between Bureau or Creditor/Furnisher.

B) Choose just one (1) saved pending item. Remember: a Round 2 letter is about one item that you already disputed in the first letter, so it should still be in "pending."

C) Choose an appropriate letter from the library. Click next and there's your letter.

If you have any last minute changes to make to the letter, this is the time to do it. Add or delete text and modify this final version of the letter.

When it's ready, save, and print. *That was easy, right?*

Who Signs The Dispute Letters?

To save time, many companies have the clients sign a limited power of attorney (included as the "Authorization for Credit Repair Action" in your Credit Repair Cloud default online agreement) so they can sign the client's name for them.

Here's what most companies do:

- If your client has signed the "Authorization for Credit Repair Action," you simply sign the client's name on their behalf. The client is already paying you for "Document Processing" and "Credit Repair Education" — so why not just send the letter for them? It's a nice service for your client and the price of a stamp is minimal.

But if you use Credit Repair Cloud…

- Use Credit Repair Cloud's Client Onboarding feature and your client will be able to choose their own electronic signature font to be automatically inserted into the letters. (Recommended)

What To Include With The Dispute Letter

For a Round 1 letter, you only need to include these 2 items: a Photo ID (like a driver's license) and Proof of Address (usually a utility bill or something official with the client's name and address). *Later rounds don't need this because you've already established that the disputes are coming from the client.

What if my client doesn't have Photo ID and Proof of Address?

Here's the full list of what is acceptable.

One item to validate ID such as:

- Valid driver's license
- Social Security card
- Pay stub
- W2 form
- 1099 form
- Court documents for legal name change
- Birth certificate
- Passport
- Marriage certificate
- Divorce decree
- State ID

- Military ID

PLUS one item to validate address such as:

- Valid driver's license
- Utility bill with the correct address (gas, water, cable, residential phone bill)
- Cell phone bill
- Pay stub
- W2 form
- 1099 form
- Rental lease agreement/house deed
- Mortgage statement
- Bank statement
- State ID

Should it be sent certified mail?

Certified mail is not mandatory, but if you have the extra funds to cover the cost it does provide an awesome paper trail and give you important timestamps that come in handy later down the road if you choose to sue the recipient.

What return address should be on the envelope?

The address on the envelope and the letter must always be your client's current address.

But how will I know when changes happen?

The credit bureaus and creditors send their replies directly to your client. Ask your client to forward all correspondence to you so you can keep their records up to date. There is no shortcut to this step. All successful credit repair companies must do this.

Pro Tip: Ask your client to take a photo of the replies with their phone and email them to you. Once you've received an update about an item, you can change the status of that item in the software or choose your next round.

Why Send Everything By Snail Mail?

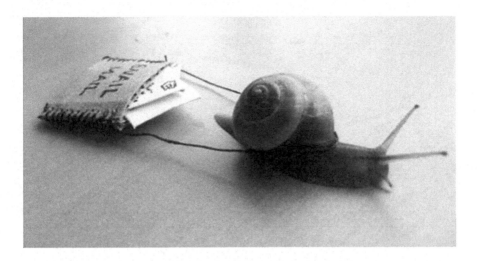

Can't I save time and submit disputes electronically?

Yes, that would be easy, but unfortunately, rushing credit bureaus is not going to get you better results — in fact, quite the opposite.

The biggest credit repair companies in America process millions of clients and they still send paper letters by snail mail. Why? Because it is time consuming for the credit bureaus to handle paper correspondence in the limited time allowed. As a result, the bureaus fight less — and so you wind up delivering better results for your clients.

The bottom line is this: Credit Repair Cloud is cutting edge, but credit repair itself is low-tech. It works best by paper mail. So for the foreseeable future, we have to overwhelm the bureaus by physically mailing the letters to them. The goal is to get the best success rate. And, after all, a high success rate will keep your customers happy — and paying!

Which Credit Bureau Address Do I Send Disputes To?

Many people ask what addresses they should be sending disputes to. Especially if a letter happens to get returned to them. Here's the dealio...

If you're using Credit Repair Cloud, you're already sending to the correct addresses. The three bureau addresses loaded into Credit Repair Cloud are the very same official addresses that the three bureaus post on their web sites.

So if a letter occasionally gets returned...don't panic.

The U.S. Postal workers have been known to make mistakes.

Bureaus have many addresses.

As long as you're sending to the same official addresses that the 3 bureaus show on their official pages, which are the same addresses we have by default in Credit Repair Cloud, rest assured that you are sending to the correct address.

How Many Disputes Can I Send At One Time?

There's a fine line between being proactive and getting on a credit bureau's "bad side." You can send as many disputes as you like, but I recommend never sending more than 5 dispute items to a credit bureau within a 30 day period. Note: the largest credit repair company in America (L.L.) only disputes **2-3 items per month**.

There are some exceptions, for example; a ton of inquiries and new accounts all due to identity theft, but generally speaking, if you send a huge laundry list of disputes all at one time, you risk your disputes being labeled as "frivolous" (which is not pleasant, trust me). After that, the bureaus can deny all of your disputes, and you'll waste more months fighting the "frivolous" accusation instead. It's far better to slow it down, especially if you're just learning the ropes. The only time to send a huge laundry list of disputes all at once is when your client is a victim of identity theft, and you can prove it with a copy of the police report.

Sending fewer disputes at a steady pace will also increase your client's life cycle — and, therefore, <u>lifetime value</u> (don't deliberately slow down the process against your client's benefit — just keep it to a pace that gives them the best success rate). A higher success rate means happier clients. And happy clients on a long life cycle are your best source for sustained revenue. *Win!*

Understanding The Date Of Last Activity

Clients will commonly have questions about the Date of Last Activity (DLA) on their credit reports. Whether you're just starting a credit repair company or are a seasoned professional, it is important to understand what a DLA is, how collections companies use it, and how it can be used to hurt your clients.

What is the DLA?

The Date of Last Activity listed on a client's credit report is updated when one of three things happens on any active account: the consumer makes a payment, misses a payment, or the balance of the account increases. The DLA used to include the "purge from" date or the date the item will be removed from the report, but this has recently changed. The "purge from" date is now a separate item on the report (and often not on the report at all).

Who controls the DLA?

The DLA is not updated by the original creditor or the debt collector; It is instead controlled by the bureaus. However, creditors and debt collectors are responsible for reporting information to the bureaus that will help them update the DLA.

How can debt collectors use a DLA to hurt consumers?

Some debt collectors have been known to make regular changes to clients' accounts, which triggers a balance increase being sent to the bureaus and changes made to the DLA. This can hurt a client's credit report. Bureaus may do this to intimidate consumers in hopes of pressuring them to pay.

How can I help my client with his/her DLA?

When combing through your client's credit report, pay special attention to the DLA. Make sure that the DLA reflects the actual date that a payment was made, missed, or the balance increased. If it is not, begin the basic dispute process to have the item changed or deleted.

Can the DLA affect when an item will eventually fall off a credit report?

No, the "original" delinquency date is what is used to determine when the item will be deleted. Contrary to popular belief, the DLA has nothing to do with when an item will be deleted from the credit report. Also, making payments on a past due account does not change the original delinquency date and does not reset the clock. So, unless the item is about to fall off the report it always pays to catch up on late payments to bring a past due account current. Collections accounts are deleted seven years from the original delinquency date of the original account. Collections accounts are always associated with the original account so they must be deleted at the same time. Additionally, the further in the past a delinquency occurred, the less impact it can have on a credit score.

As a credit repair professional, remaining informed about updates and changes in the credit repair landscape is crucial. By staying up to date about the DLA and other information, you will be able to serve as a trusted advisor and help your clients reach their credit goals.

How To Get A Goodwill Deletion

When starting a credit repair company, it is easy to get so caught up in the "us vs. them" mentality that you forget one of the first things you learned as a child: *ask nicely*.

In many cases, creditors will perform a "goodwill deletion" and remove negative items even If they are accurate.

How does this work and how can you use it to help your clients?

The goodwill deletion request letter is based on the age-old principle that everyone makes mistakes. It is, simply put, the practice of admitting a mistake to a lender and asking them not to penalize you for it. Obviously, this usually works only with one-time, low-level items like 30-day late payments.

In today's credit environment, the clock for a 30-day late payment begins at the debt's due date. So it is unlikely that the client could get away with the excuse that they were on vacation, working long hours, or that they only paid a day or two late. Instead, the client should base his/her request for a goodwill deletion on the fact that this was a one-time mistake, an anomaly that won't be repeated. This works best if the credit payment history is good and there is little evidence of past mistakes.

A request letter for a goodwill deletion should be worded quite differently from your typical dispute letter. Instead of firm and professional, it should be approachable and apologetic. The client should admit that he or she was late, but insist that he or she is typically a reliable client of X years and will not continue to make the same mistake. This strategy does actually work and is a great tool for your clients who have good credit histories with just a few errors.

You'll find a great letter for this in the section for Sample Dispute Letters. Or, of you're a Credit Repair Cloud user, you will find this in your library. It's called "Goodwill Letter sent to Original Creditor," and you can easily modify it to fit any scenario.

This strategy is most successful when the letter is sent to the original creditor, not to the credit bureau. Bureaus are not likely to grant goodwill deletions, as they see them as creating inaccurate credit scores. Clients have more pull with creditors with whom they have existing relationships, regular payments, and the motivation to keep a long-time customer happy. Goodwill deletions are a great option for clients who have made one or two small errors on an account, but have an otherwise good history. It is a great tool to offer clients when these accurate items cannot otherwise be deleted.

Advanced Tactics/Removing Difficult Items

Beyond The Basics

Often, a valid dispute will be denied by the credit bureaus on the basis that they performed an "investigation" and the item was "verified." To understand why this happens and how to get past it, you have to understand how information is submitted onto consumers' credit reports.

Creditors submit information to credit bureaus via an online portal. This information is populated every time a credit report is pulled. When a dispute is submitted, the bureau will compare the information against the original submission from the creditor to verify its validity. Essentially, the bureau **compares false information against itself** and verifies that it is the same — concluding that the information must be true.

To make matters worse, bureaus may flag continued attempts to have these items removed as "frivolous" and refuse to investigate further. This circular reasoning is not only very frustrating, but also a violation of the Fair Credit Reporting Act (FCRA).

Do not let the bureaus intimidate you into giving up!

The FCRA gives consumers the right to have false information modified or removed from their credit reports. There are several advanced strategies you can employ on behalf of a credit repair client in order to have these items removed.

Action Plan Overview

Step 1: Determine what reasoning the bureau used to deny the dispute.

Step 2: Based on the reasoning, follow up with a corresponding response in an attempt to have the bureau open a new investigation.

Step 3: If the request is still denied, submit complaints to the government agencies that regulate the bureaus. Remember to inform the bureau that these complaints were submitted.

Step 4: Consult an attorney to discuss pursuing a lawsuit.

Possible Responses From Credit Bureaus

After submitting your original request, the credit bureau has up to 30 days to investigate a dispute. After the investigation period, the client will receive a response that either the dispute was successful and the item was deleted, or that the dispute was denied based on one of the following reasons:

The Item Was Verified And Will Remain On The Report

If a dispute is denied because the item was verified, draft a follow-up letter with different language from the first one, explaining why the item should be removed. It is important that this sounds genuine and not like it is coming from a credit repair company. Then, use one of the methods below to pursue a new investigation:

Submit Proof

Send a dispute letter with every piece of documentation that the client has on why the item is inaccurate, incomplete, or unverifiable. This can include the client's credit report from other credit bureaus with the correct information. Draft a letter explaining clearly why the item should be modified or removed and reference the included supporting documentation.

Request Proof From The Creditor

Creditors must have documented proof of a debt for that debt to be included on a client's credit report. Write to the creditor requesting proof of both the original debt agreement (signed credit or loan application) and payment history. The creditor will have 15 days to respond to this request with proof. If proof is unavailable, the item must be deleted from the credit report.

Request Information On Method Of Verification

Send another dispute letter asking the bureau to explain how they verified the item. Remember to send it via certified mail, as the bureau must respond within 15 days of receipt. Once you receive a response, you will have a clearer picture of how to dispute the item further.

Dispute The E-Oscar System

When a dispute is submitted, the bureau's e-Oscar converts the dispute into one of twenty-six two-digit codes, which are then transmitted to the creditor for verification. These codes include things like "item incorrect" or "information missing." The creditor then checks this information based on its records and submits another code back to the bureau stating whether the item was verified. Bureaus are required to adhere to FCRA, not e-Oscar. You can consider submitting a letter disputing the use of this system and requesting that the item be verified manually.

Contact The Bureau's Legal Department

Write a letter directly to the bureau's legal department re-stating your request and your belief that the bureau is in violation of the FCRA by inadequately investigating the dispute. Request information on how the investigation was made, including any forms that were filled out and the contact information on the creditor that was contacted to verify the information.

Consult An Attorney

If one or more of these methods failed to elicit a favorable response, write to the bureau informing them that you have consulted an attorney and found them to be willfully noncompliant with the FCRA. In many cases, this type of letter will cause the bureau to open an investigation, as they believe you may pursue a lawsuit. Remember to keep copies of every piece of correspondence sent or received. If a lawsuit becomes necessary, you will need proof that you have exhausted all methods to have the bureau respond to your dispute.

*Pro Tip: There are attorneys who specialize in credit and many will work on contingency: meaning they will not charge the client anything. They may even give you a finder's fee. So make friends with a good credit attorney in your area and build a great relationship with them.

The Bureau Requests Additional Information

Bureaus will typically request additional information (even if you have already provided it) as a stall tactic. If you have previously sent this information respond with all of the documentation, including proof of identity. Assert that this information has already been submitted and this is the <u>last time</u> you will send it before filing a complaint.

"Your Letter Was Suspicious"

This is a very common stall tactic. Investigations cost bureaus money, so they hope to intimidate customers into dropping their disputes by responding that the dispute letter was "suspicious." You will often see this response if you've forgotten to include your client's ID docs with the Round 1 letter.

*Pro Tip: When this happens, resend the same letter on behalf of the client with a note that says; "Yes I sent this dispute, and I am now attaching my photo ID and proof of address so you can see it is me." You might also reiterate that this is a legitimate request and by ignoring it the bureau is in violation of the FCRA, and this time include the ID docs.

"The Dispute Is Frivolous"

Under the FCRA, credit bureaus have a right to dismiss your dispute if they believe it to be frivolous or not serious. If this is the case, respond with a letter requesting a reason for why they believe this to be the case and ask what you need to do to have the matter investigated. You can also send a letter directly to the manager of the bureau's customer relations department explaining the situation. This will often lead the bureau to think you are considering legal action, which will trigger an investigation into your request.

*Pro Tip: You will most often see the "frivolous" response if you've sent way too many disputes to one bureau at one time. It's just not believable. That's why experts recommend sending fewer than 5 disputes per bureau, per month (and 2-3 is even better). Fly low and avoid the radar.

"We Suspect You Are Working With A Credit Repair Company."

Credit bureaus may refuse to investigate a client's request on the basis they believe he/she is working with a credit repair company. If this is the case, send a letter on behalf of the client saying that the bureau cannot prove this is the case, and refusing to investigate without proof is a violation of the FCRA. You can also inform the FTC that the bureau is refusing to investigate, and enclose a copy of that letter with your follow-up to the bureau. Additionally, it's perfectly legal for a consumer to work with a credit repair company. This is just a stall tactic.

Reporting Credit Bureau Violations

There are several US government agencies that have a stake in the compliance of credit bureaus to regulations. If a bureau is noncompliant or slow to respond, you can send a letter any or all of the following agencies. Include in your letter copies of all past correspondence. Remember to forward copies of these letters to the bureau so they understand the seriousness of your request.

- The Federal Trade Commission
- The Office of the Attorney General
- State Regulatory Agencies
- Federal Reserve System
- Federal Deposit Insurance Corporation
- Comptroller of the Currency
- Credit and Insurance

Still No Response?

Credit bureaus have 30 days to respond to your request. If after this period the bureau still has not favorably responded to your request, consider consulting an attorney to discuss pursuing a lawsuit for a violation of the FCRA. This is why it is very important to have copies of all correspondence with tracking numbers. Send the bureau a letter stating that you are considering legal action. This fact alone might push them to open an investigation.

Becoming An Expert On Debt Collection Practices

How to Strike Back Against Debt Collectors and Win!

From time to time you will inevitably be approached by clients who were contacted by debt collectors. There are several federal laws and regulations, primarily the Fair Debt Collection Practices Act (FDCPA), and state mirror laws that protect consumers from being harassed or abused by debt collectors. The FDCPA was created to prevent unfair, deceptive, or abusive practices by debt collectors. Many debt collectors break the law. When they do, it's possible not only to stop the harassment, but also to be awarded a settlement.

In your ongoing effort to become an expert in all things credit repair, it is important to understand these regulations so you are able to advise clients on how to respond and whether they are being treated unfairly. As your credit repair business grows, we recommend building a relationship with a local law firm that specializes in debt collection so you can work together to help your clients repair their credit.

The FDCPA includes three major debt collector restrictions that could affect your clients. These are explained below with examples of each:

1. **Harassment or abuse:**

   A debt collector may not do or say anything that leads to harassment, oppression, or abuse. This includes making threats to individual safety, income, freedom, or employment. Examples: A debt collector cannot use abusive or obscene language. They cannot call before 8 a.m. or after 9 p.m. unless you agree.They cannot call you at work if you have asked them not to, and they cannot speak with anyone else (other than your attorney) about the debt. They also may not threaten to publish a debtor's name publicly as someone who doesn't pay bills.

2. **False or misleading representations:**

   A debt collector may not represent themselves in a deceptive or misleading way. They must be clear that they are debt collectors and are contacting the individual for the purpose of collecting debt. Especially relevant to your clients: Debt collectors must communicate that a disputed debt is being disputed. Examples: A debt collector that sends communication or makes phone calls claiming to be calling from a government agency, attorney, law enforcement, or a credit bureau representative in order to get information or payment would be in violation of the FDCPA.

3. **Unfair practices:**

   A debt collector cannot use any unfair or outrageous means to collect a debt. This includes adding or causing a debtor to incur fees that were not part of the original debt agreement. Example: A debt collector may not collect extra fees or interest from the debtor for any reason.

Once a client receives an initial letter of communication from a debt collector (called a "Dunning" letter), he or she has thirty days to respond to dispute the validity of the debt or request verification of the debt. Either of these actions will trigger a stop in all communications from debt collectors while the debt is being investigated. Remember that disputing the debt will not make it disappear. It is important to give your clients a clear picture of what to expect in the debt dispute process.

Now that you understand the basics of the FDCPA, it is important to know how you, as a credit repair professional, should advise your clients to proceed when treated unfairly by a debt collector.

The most important thing is to collect all communications that your client has received from debt collectors. This can be most easily done through your credit repair software. When teaching clients how to upload documents to their client portal, encourage them to upload everything they have received from debt collectors. Quick and easy access to all documents related to debt collection — and later possible dispute or verification — is crucial to the process.

It's also important for the client to take notes during any phone conversations with a debt collector, write down the time and date of any calls, and keep copies of any voicemails received. This type of record keeping will become critical evidence if the collection agent has broken any laws.

Additionally, here are 6 ways that your client can strike back against a debt collector who is violating the law:

1. Report the debt collector to a Government Agency. For example: The FTC at www.ftccomplaintassistant.gov or the CFPB at www.consumerfinance.gov/complaint.

2. Report the violations to the State Attorney General, because the debt collector is most likely violating State laws as well.

3. Sue the debt collector in small claims court.

4. Sue the debt collector in state court.

5. Use this violation as leverage in a debt settlement negotiation. Debt collectors know how costly a FDCPA lawsuit can be for them, so they

may be more likely to settle the debt.

6. Consult with a law firm that specializes in debt collection.

As your credit repair business grows, we recommend cultivating a partnership with a law firm that specializes in debt collection. Skilled attorneys will comb through all communication received from debt collectors looking for violations that can be used to dispute or remove the debt. They will interview your client to understand the debt, examine the credit report for violations, and contact the debt collectors on the client's behalf. In most situations, these law firms will collect their fees only if the case is won, at no cost to you or your clients.

When dealing with debt collectors, it's important to keep in mind that FDCPA only applies to personal or household debt accumulated by individual consumers. The guidelines do not apply to any type of business debt. Secondly, "communications" from debt collectors can refer to any direct or indirect contact, including posting information to individuals' credit reports. Finally, in the FDCPA a "debt collector" refers to any person or company who regularly collects debt. This usually does not include the original creditor.

As a credit repair professional, you are a trusted advisor to your clients on all things related to their credit and debt. Understanding and having the ability to advise on the FDCPA is a crucial part of this process. By collecting the necessary information and having easy access to attorneys that will help your clients reach their goals, you will position yourself as an expert in your field.

How Do I Erase A Bankruptcy?

I get asked this question a lot. First off, please remember that we're a software company only and not allowed to give legal advice, and you should always consult with an attorney for legal advice. That being said, here's some general information about how to help a client who has a bankruptcy:

Bankruptcies are court records that stay on the credit report for 10 years. They generally don't appear out of nowhere by themselves.

If there is a bankruptcy on your client's report, chances are it is because your client requested that bankruptcy and he/she paid an attorney a lot of money to file it for them — most likely to wipe out their giant bills. If your client does not know how the bankruptcy got onto his report, and if it's truly an error, you would simply dispute it to the bureau just like any other error.

But if the bankruptcy is real, it's very difficult to remove real court records. So it's important to be honest with your clients so they will have realistic expectations, and to never promise things that are not possible (like removing court records that are real). That being said, there are ways that people do remove bankruptcies from credit reports. These do change over time, that's why I did not include them in the book, but you can see the latest secrets for bankruptcy removal on my podcast at **CreditRepairCloud.com/YouTube**.

Here are some additional ways that you CAN help a client who has a bankruptcy:

- Look on the report for creditors who are still showing a balance that should have been wiped to zero in the bankruptcy. It's very common to find them still on the report.

- If you're a Credit Repair Cloud user, you can dispute those items to the bureau using the wizard dropdown reasons that say "this item was included in a bankruptcy, balance should be zero." That will help your client and improve the credit report.That looks like this:

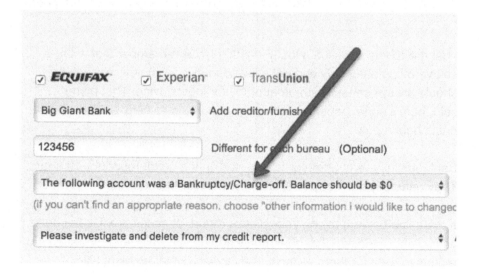

But, in the case of a very old bankruptcy:

- The creditors should have already fallen off after seven years.

- An old bankruptcy that is about to fall off by itself won't carry as much weight on the score as a new bankruptcy.

- It's going to fall off the report by itself after 10 years.

The Business Of Credit Repair

10 Tips From Experts On Starting A Credit Repair Business

With any new business, it's nice to have help from someone who's been there. So we asked a group of expert credit repair professionals for the top tips they give to people considering entering the industry:

1. **Credit Repair is NOT a part-time job**

   So many people think they can do credit repair one or two days a week on top of their current full-time job. This is almost never successful. Clients and prospects will not take you seriously if you're only reachable a few hours a week. If starting a credit repair business is something you are serious about, and you want to build a profitable business, work towards making it a full-time job.

2. **Create a business plan**

   The "start first, think later" method is never a good idea when starting any kind of new business. Before even reaching out to your first prospect, make sure you have a well-developed business plan in place. It should cover the 4 basic parts of starting a new business: Finance, sales, marketing, and operations. This is a great opportunity to reach out to other small business owners to ask for advice and begin building relationships. Keep in mind that you don't have to spend any money to do marketing. It can all be done with relationships. Watch our "How to Start a Credit Repair Business" webinar and you'll get plenty of ideas. You'd find it on our blog at www.creditrepaircloud.com/blog or visit https://www.youtube.com/watch?v=qLQUkn87tew

3. **Identify your niche**

Before you get started, you should identify which types of potential clients you are hoping to target. This will affect your affiliate, marketing, and operational strategies. For example, you might start by targeting people who have been recently turned down for mortgages whose FICO scores are above 540 but less than 620. This will give you a target range so you can easily decide who is and is not a potential client. Taking on clients who you simply cannot help to achieve their goals is a losing game.

4. **Learn, learn, learn**

In many ways, you are the product you are selling. People need to feel like you are an expert who can advise them on a very personal and confusing issue. The more you know about credit repair, the better able you will be to teach your clients what they need to know. Read as much as you can about credit repair strategies, history, and the industry. Attend events, build relationships with other credit repair professionals, etc. Ongoing personal education will help your business thrive. Additionally, read our blog (for weekly credit repair business tips) and read our many free guides.

5. **Delegate where possible**

It can be so difficult for small business owners to give up control. After all, they have single-handedly launched this business from the ground up. However, you can't do it all. Fatigue will set in and you will start to let things fall through the cracks. Additionally, working with people with different skill sets will strengthen your business. If you're a great long-term planner but not so good with the day-to-day, hire an operations guru who can help you with the details. At the very least, if you're overwhelmed — get an assistant.

6. **Build affiliate relationships**

Our experts agree that one of the fastest ways to get clients and scale your business is to build strong affiliate partnerships. Mortgage brokers, car dealers, and other lenders make amazing referral partners. They want to see your business succeed so that they can complete a sale to a customer they otherwise would have had to turn away. Focus on creating these relationships in the initial stages of launching your business.

7. **Educate affiliate partners**

As we mentioned above, affiliate partners are an amazing resource. However, they are not nearly as strong when they are uneducated on how your services work and what types of leads you are looking for. Let them in on the "niche" we discussed above so they don't spend time sending you unrealistic leads. It also helps to provide them with an education packet so they know how to talk about your business to potential leads.

8. **Create a thoughtful pricing structure**

Many people decide on a pricing structure based on their competitors' prices. This is often unsuccessful as it does not consider what will actually make your company profitable. Figure out your Cost per Acquisition based on the time, money, and resources you've spent acquiring leads. Base your audit fee on this figure so that you know you will always start out with a profit. For example, if your CPA is $89 your audit fee should be greater than that.

9. **Have an operational system in place**

Before you talk to your first client, you must have a clear, transparent operational system in place. This should include your client intake process, how you will pull credit reports, when clients will be charged, email automation, etc. This will make your life so much easier in the long run and will make your business appear professional to outsiders.

10. Educate your clients

Your clients look up to you to be the expert. Let's face it, the actual "work" of repairing credit is minimal. Once a client is set up in the system, it's about five minutes of work per month to manage each client. Go the extra mile by educating your clients on how credit works, how they can help speed up the credit repair process, pay down balances, and stop applying for credit. Most importantly: help them change their credit and debt habits, so they can maintain their great credit long after your work is done. These little extras that are very easy for you will give your clients the "wow" factor that will make them want to tell all their friends how much you helped them. This personal touch is what grows a business like wildfire.

Getting Started With A Credit Repair Business

Get a copy of your own credit report to study

You are entitled to one free copy a year from each of the three major bureaus: Equifax, Experian and TransUnion.

Learn as much as you can about the credit reporting system

Read the first few chapters on credit repair basics. Read the Fair Credit Reporting Act section. Also see our blogs and other free resources on our site at www.creditrepaircloud.com.

Understand your role in the process

Once you obtain your client's credit reports, you can then work with that client to correct any mistakes, acting as the intermediary between them and the credit bureau or creditor.

Understand what you are selling and be careful what you promise.

A credit repair company cannot "erase" negative items that are accurate and have been present on a credit report for less than seven years. However, many accurate but negative items can be removed with a bit of finesse if you learn the right negotiating tactics and approach the creditors and collection agencies in the proper manner. Here is the good news: 79% of all credit reports contain errors. This means that MOST credit reports contain errors.Those errors come off very easily with a few clicks of your mouse. Simply removing errors will improve a score almost immediately. Once you've accomplished that, you can further enhance a credit report by negotiating the remaining negative items.

Work smarter, not harder

The most common mistake entrepreneurs make is in managing their time poorly. Time spent creating dispute letters and handling paperwork can eat up hundreds of hours and drop your hourly earnings very low. This is

where software comes in handy. It can help you to work "smart" —
saving you hundreds of hours by automating the process and giving you
more off-time to enjoy your success.

Understand that it's a "people business."

You must be good at working with people. After all, your clients are real
people. You must be a good listener and you must have rapport with
them. You must also be good at building alliances with other businesses
who will refer clients to you.

Promote and market your business

Now that you have everything in place, it is time to start promoting and
marketing your credit consulting business. You might look up local and
national credit repair businesses to get an idea of the services they offer
and the types of fees associated with these services.

Some credit repair specialists don't charge fees at all. For mortgage
brokers and auto dealers, generating leads and closing more loans is
worth more than any fee. Go through all the information you can find,
decide on your fees and services, and get ready to advertise.

It's easy to create credit repair business flyers and business cards, either
professionally or on your home computer. On the flyers, give a brief
description about your services and contact information. Remember:
Less is more. Post these flyers everywhere you can. You may also want
to place small ads for your services in local newspapers, church
newsletters, periodicals and with local merchants who deal with
financing: mortgage brokers, real estate agents, auto dealers, etc.

Offer friends and family your credit repair counseling services for free,
and then ask them for a letter of recommendation. This will quickly help
to build your client base. Word of mouth is the very best kind of
advertising.

You may want to consider giving credit repair and debt seminars and
classes to help people help themselves before they are too far in debt.

Perhaps you might want to give talks at high schools and colleges about ways to stay out of debt. The students will go home with the information you have given them and your business card or brochure, and tell their parents, who may end up as your next clients.

Start small and work out the kinks before trying to expand too quickly

As a credit consultant, you should start to build your business locally before expanding too fast or going to the Internet. If you build your credibility early, when you branch out, you will have experience and a history of customer satisfaction to back you up.

Stay honest with your clients. You are providing them with a very important service. They must trust you and your business. Credit repair can be confusing to many. Reassure and give them the information they want. This will enhance your credibility and increase your credit repair business well into the future.

Don't try to pretend that you are a large company. Be small and proud. Be the boutique service who will go the extra mile.

Running a credit repair business can be made simpler with the help of software. Credit Repair Cloud stores your client information to merge into its database of letters, saving you many long hours of letter writing and reducing it to just a few clicks. It's also designed to grow and scale your business faster.

Don't Reinvent The Wheel

Planning a Credit Repair Business? You should study proven business models first. Study the biggest players. You know them. The very biggest has the initials LL — and there are a few others who are generating hundreds of millions of dollars in revenue. Look at their sites, their simple pricing plans and the similarities — but NEVER copy any text or images from their site or you'll get to know their attorneys. Just look and gather ideas. Yes, they are making millions. You can, too. Just take it one step at a time.

Concentrate on keeping your clients happy and remember that simplicity is the key to scaling later. Structure your business in a simple way, with simple pricing and you'll quickly have your piece of the pie.

How Much Should I Charge My Clients?

The sky's the limit — but in this business, you might actually make more by charging less. Remember: the goal is to "scale" your business. How do you do that? Slowly and methodically, with reasonable pricing, good service, and happy clients who keep your service for a very long time (and tell their friends). Visit the Credit Repair Business ROI Calculator at www.creditrepaircloud.com/calculator and run some pricing projections.

Yes, but how much should I charge?

People charge in different ways: flat fee, pay per deletion, etc. But of all the methods we see, charging a one-time "first work" fee followed one month later by affordable, recurring monthly payments is always the ticket to high revenue. Since each client takes less than 5 minutes of processing per month (after setup), a small reasonable monthly fee is appropriate. Then just focus on getting more and more clients. Give them awesome service and educate your clients on how to better manage their credit — and you'll have lifelong happy customers.

Determining the exact fee to charge depends on your clientele, but here's a hint: visit the websites of the largest credit repair companies. They are making millions, so why reinvent the wheel? Just don't copy any text or images from their site unless you're dying to get to know their legal department.

Closing Sales

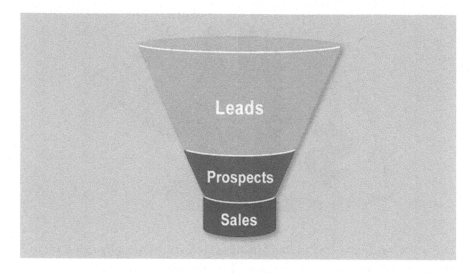

Congratulations! After a successful marketing and outreach campaign you've found a prospect that is interested in becoming a client.

Many people who are new to credit repair focus primarily on sales and credit repair, but do not have a process for actually converting a lead to a prospect and finally to a client. This should be a smooth and seamless process that gathers all necessary information without wasting your valuable time.

Step 1: Gauge a prospect's interest and timeframe

Give a brief overview of your services, but otherwise listen to the prospect's story. This is a great time to gauge their goals, pain points, and whether or not the prospect is a fit for your services. Make sure you walk away from the initial meeting with a realistic goal and timeframe. If the prospect is looking to buy a home in 30 days, it may not be worth moving forward to the initial consultation.

Step 2: Get a copy of the prospect's credit report

There are several different ways that you can get a copy of a potential client's credit report. Our experts recommend helping prospects pull the report themselves with their own credit/debit card. Typically this costs the client $1. When the client orders their own report, they do not suffer a hit to their score. Have a very clear process in place for this, whether it be through an automated email, webinar, or in a meeting. The quicker you can get a copy of the credit report, the sooner you will be able to convert the prospect to a client.

Step 3: Perform a consultation

This is best in person or over zoom, because it is visual. Once you have a copy of the prospect's credit report, you will be able to quickly go through it to determine whether the client is a good fit for your services. We recommend having a checklist that you can fill out to ensure you can quickly grab all relevant information. Your consultation should include 2 primary buckets:

1. The hard facts: How many derogatory accounts, collection accounts, inquiries, and incidences of incorrect personal information exist on the credit report.
2. The client's goal and timeframe: If you were unable to determine this information in Step 1, make sure you know it before converting a prospect. If you agree to help a client buy a car only to later find out they want to make the purchase next week, you will have a very unsatisfied customer on your hands. Be very clear about what you can and cannot offer and a reasonable timeframe.

The biggest mistake we see credit repair professionals make in this step is spending too much time on the details. DO NOT confuse the initial consultation with the audit. You should not be spending a large amount of time on a free consultation.

Step 4: Determine the Prospect's Eligibility

Based on your initial conversations and consultation, determine whether or not the individual is a good fit for your program. Make sure that the prospect's timeframe and expectations are reasonable, and that there are items you are able to dispute on the credit report.

Whether or not you choose to accept the prospect as a client, make sure to document the reasoning behind your decision. This is helpful for your own purposes of creating defined selection criteria, and is helpful in the case of a government audit.

Step 5: Perform the audit

Again this is visual, so this is the point in the process where you can sit down with the client (either virtually or in person) to sift through the details of his credit report. Write down every piece of inaccurate information and ask the client to weigh in on what should be disputed and in what order. Getting the client involved in the process will ensure that he has a reasonable expectation for what to expect and is ready for the next steps.

Step 6: Make a plan

After performing the audit make a detailed action plan and share it with the client. Make sure that he understands what you will do and what he can expect. If you have any collateral materials describing the process, share them at this time so the client feels prepared. This is also a great time to suggest any ancillary services that you or your affiliate partners might be able to provide to benefit his financial situation.

Regardless of whether your credit repair company has one employee or 100, creating and implementing a clear process for converting prospects to clients will help reduce inefficiencies and provide more opportunities for business growth. The steps listed here are a great outline of what the steps this process should contain, but remember to customize your methods to best fit your company's needs.

Growing Your Business By Building Trust

We've all seen successful credit repair businesses and wondered whether they had discovered the secret to sales or if they were just supremely lucky. More often than not, their success can be attributed to having a solid marketing and sales strategy.

Identifying the problem

It is not a secret that there is a huge credit problem in the United States. More than 25% of Americans have a credit score below 599 and almost two-thirds of Americans identify as "always or usually" living paycheck-to-paycheck. Because of this, home-ownership is declining, and Americans are unable to access the financing they need to make large purchases. Whether this crisis is due to consumer irresponsibility or predatory lending ultimately doesn't matter. What does matter to you and your clients is finding a solution to their individual problems. As a credit repair consultant, your role is to counsel customers and provide the advice, education, and resources to access credit for which they wouldn't normally be approved.

Asking the right questions

Clients can sense fairly quickly whether you are approaching them to make money and close a deal or if you are sincerely interested in helping them. If you want to have the right relationship with your clients, you have to be in it for the right reasons. Think of yourself as a trusted advisor and focus on building trust. Make sure you are asking the right questions: What happened? How did it happen? How long has it been going on?

What are your goals?

Trust goes both ways, so it is also important to tell your clients about yourself. People don't buy what you do, they buy how and why you do it. Explain to them why you got into the credit repair business. Sell people on your passion and authenticity, and they will trust you to help them with their problems. People with credit problems are often taken advantage of, so offer them not only your credit repair services, but also educational materials and resources to help them help themselves.

Creating your marketing strategy

By focusing on building trust and asking the right questions, you can build a simple, targeted marketing and sales strategy. People often know what their problem is but need to be educated on the solution. *Do you need help getting back on track? Need a new car? Tired of renting? Have you been denied? Bad credit?* We can help. Who you target depends on your passion and purpose. Remember the standard sales and marketing funnel (attract, engage, nurture, sell, deliver), but also remember that every business is different. Your funnel may be different based on your personal philosophy, and that's okay.

Taking advantage of credit repair software

Credit Repair Cloud can take a lot of the heavy lifting out of engaging and building trust with potential clients through automation features. If you automate your system the right way, customers will already know about your personal beliefs and passions, how you may be able to help them, and why they should trust you — before you even have an initial conversation. Successful automation should include the following steps:

1. **A landing page:** When a potential client clicks on an ad, they should be taken to the web lead form on your site where they can enter their contact information — and you will receive a lead in your Credit Repair Cloud for your sales team to follow up.

2. **An introductory email:** Once a client requests more information through your landing page, they should receive a welcome email from you. This should inform them about credit repair in general, but more specifically about why you got into credit repair and why you feel passionate about helping people. This will set you apart from others in the industry and begin building trust.

3. **An educational email:** After a day or two, follow up with an email that includes educational resources. Clients will feel that you are not just trying to sell to them but sincerely want to help them with their situation. Even if they don't sign up with you, you still want to provide the resources to help them help themselves.

Closing the deal

Continue to follow up with occasional emails to build trust. Even if that particular client does not sign up for your services, you will be at the top of mind if they or someone in their network needs credit repair in the future.

Ultimately, the goal is to invite the client to a free consultation where you will explain the credit repair process, how the bureaus work, give them a general timeline, help them order a credit report, import their report into Credit Repair Cloud to create an audit report. walk through the audit report with them, and encourage them to start services. Be honest and realistic. Be affordable and never promise things you cannot deliver.

Be transparent

Remember that credit repair is a "people business." You're not doing anything that they cannot do for themselves, but you're doing it in a more organized manner because you have software to save you time and keep you organized. You also have a better sense of the law and how things work. This makes you the trusted expert.

Each time you work in Credit Repair Cloud, your client will be notified of changes and updates. They can log into their portal to see your progress, and it makes the entire process transparent, with no secrets. Transparency builds trust.

Educate your clients

We will say this again and again: Credit Repair is 10% document processing and 90% credit education. The actual "work" per client is minimal: a few mouse clicks and the cost of a stamp. Your more important task is to educate your client to change their credit habits, to pay bills down to below 25% of the credit line, and to stop applying for credit. Those three things alone will increase the score, and that's only the beginning.

Building Integrity In The Credit Repair Industry

How to build a culture of integrity

A cursory Internet search for "Credit Repair Scam" will turn up thousands of results containing stories of people who were taken advantage of in the name of credit repair. This is such a problem in our industry that many credit repair professionals have begun calling themselves "Credit Coaches" or "Credit Counselors" in an attempt to get around the stigma of credit repair. Many of the scams discussed on message boards and Internet forums are not, in fact, credit repair companies. The role of credit repair companies is to make sure that our clients are being adequately represented and getting a fair deal as is laid out in credit laws.

One organization that is trying to change this stigma is the National Association of Credit Services Organizations (NACSO). NACSO, founded in 2007 in Washington DC, advocates for fair and ethical business practices in the credit repair industry. Some credit repair companies choose to become a member of NACSO to lend more legitimacy to their business and to help change the story around the credit repair industry.

There are several ways that individual credit repair professionals can begin to change the negative public view of the industry. The first, and most obvious of which, is to simply operate your business in the most ethical, transparent way possible. Hold yourself and your employees to a high standard. Educate your employees about operating with integrity and create a public ethics statement that is featured prominently on your website. This will help build trust with your clients and help raise the reputation of the industry as a whole.

One common ethical barrier that all credit report professionals face is a client claiming identity theft. When going over clients' credit reports, some may claim that they are not responsible for some of the debt listed. Whether you believe the client or not, it is important not to put yourself in the middle of this claim. As a credit repair professional, you can advise your client to file a police report and submit this report to the credit bureaus. You can offer resources on how to do this through the

"Resources" portal on your credit repair software. You should not, however, get involved by filing the report on your clients' behalf. If it were to become clear after you filed the report that your client was lying about the debt, your company would be held in violation of the law for filing a false report. Filing a claim on behalf of a client is one practice that many credit repair companies may not even know is both unethical and potentially illegal. Educate yourself and your employees on integrity and best practices to avoid a sticky situation.

Finally, you can help change the public face of credit repair by getting involved in the conversation. Get active on social media. When you see people talking negatively about credit repair, say something. Explain that credit repair companies like yours are just trying to help people get back on their feet after their credit has been negatively impacted. By holding yourself to a high standard and spreading the word about your own integrity, you can begin to build trust to grow your own business and for the entire credit repair industry.

Ignore Old Wives' Tales

In the credit forums where lonely trolls lurk to argue about credit, you'll hear some outrageous whoppers:

- "Write dispute letters in different fonts and different colors."
- "Use colored paper."
- "Use a 'word spinner' to jumble the words and trick 'the system.'"
- "One company's credit reports and scores are more accurate than another's."

These are all silly wives tales. Just because someone wrote it on the Internet doesn't make it true.

We have some very big companies using our software. Our top users all agree: Credit repair isn't about tricking the system. It's about using the law in your favor and stating "facts." It's knowing that 8 out of 10 reports have errors and the errors will come off the easiest. It's about helping victims of identity theft. It's about educating your clients to handle their finances differently. It's about doing a service for your community. Yes, you can often remove items that are accurate, but it won't be by a trick.

Our most successful users don't pay attention to old wives' tales. They know the only things that matter are these facts:

- Try to dispute fewer than 5 items per month so your letters won't be thrown out as "frivolous."

- The biggest Credit Repair Company in America disputes only two to three items per month.

- If items come back as "verified," challenge the verification.

- Sometimes, you may negotiate an accurate item's deletion.

The pros all understand that half the job is educating clients to pay down balances, keep credit card spending below 30% of the credit line, and stop applying for new credit.

The color of the ink, the style of the font, or the color of your socks and what you've had for breakfast have ZERO bearing on the success of the dispute letter.

In the great scheme of things, the only credit bureaus that matter are Equifax, Experian and TransUnion. Any service that offers tri-merge reports, scores, and credit monitoring is a reseller of data for the credit bureaus. The only reason reports could be different from one to another is that a score can fluctuate daily, depending on the status of your accounts.

The other fascinating thing we learned from the largest companies in credit repair: They do not care about credit scores. Scores are irrelevant. What truly matters is that you correct the errors. That's what you're being paid to do — and to educate the client to change their habits so they don't end up in trouble again. If you do those two things, the scores will come up all by themselves.

5 Things A Credit Repair Company Should Know About Business Credit

"Business credit" is credit that's linked to a business' EIN number, not the owner's social security number. Every highly successful publicly owned and private company in the United States has business credit, it's how they get large amounts of credit and money without their CEOs or owners needing to supply a personal guarantee.

Even though this type of corporate credit is used by the largest businesses in the country, most entrepreneurs don't know that any business of any size can actually obtain corporate credit. Even startup businesses can build business credit as long as they know and understand the steps to do so.

For credit repair companies this is very important because, on average, 25% and sometimes more of the clients you talk to also own businesses. This means that while they are having their credit improved, customers can also be quickly building a separate credit profile for their business and obtaining credit that's not linked to their personal credit.

Business credit provides many benefits to entrepreneurs. Here are five essential things you should know about corporate credit.

#1 — Business Credit is Not Linked to Personal Credit

Business credit is credit for a business, linked to the business' EIN number, not the social security number of the business owner. This means that, when done properly, business credit can be built without the SSN number even being supplied on the credit application.

With even a little business credit established, a business owner can start getting approved for store credit cards at most major stores. When applying, they can leave their social security number off of the application — in which case, the credit issuer then pulls the EIN credit report instead.

With the credit issuer seeing a business' established tradelines, a business credit score, and a business credit profile, credit card approval could be issued based on the EIN credit, not even looking at the personal credit report.

Without a personal credit check, personal credit quality is not a factor at all in the approval decision. These business accounts won't even impact the consumer credit score.

#2 — Business Credit Scores are Mostly Based on One Factor Only

There are many different credit scores in the business world. The most common of them is the Paydex score from Dun & Bradstreet. Another is the Equifax Commercial's primary score. Both are solely based on one factor: payment history.

So all that's required to get a good business credit score is to get approved for accounts that report to the business reporting agencies and to pay those accounts as agreed. And you can accomplish this even as a startup business within 60 days.

Let's take a look at how the most popular score in the business world, the Paydex score from Dun & Bradstreet, is actually calculated:

- Expect payment to come early — 100

- Payment is prompt — 80
- Payment comes 14 days beyond terms — 70
- Payment comes 21 days beyond terms — 60
- Payment comes 30 days beyond terms — 50
- Payment comes 60 days beyond terms — 40
- Payment comes 90 days beyond terms — 30
- Payment comes 120 days beyond terms — 20

As you can see, it's solely based on payment history, making it easy to control and fast to build. This is just one of a multitude of benefits that business credit provides.

#3 — Business credit cards have no personal risk but very high limits

One of the biggest benefits of business credit is that the business owner doesn't need to personally guarantee their business debts. This means that if the owner ever goes late on an account or defaults, their personal assets can't be pursued for collection — only the business assets can.

This is important as it separates the business' liability from that of the business owner. It's also important because it keeps the owner's assets secure no matter what happens within the business. If given a choice, almost all business owners would rather not personally guarantee their business debts. And although this isn't always possible, with business credit it is.

And credit limits on business credit cards are much higher than with consumer cards. SBA states that limits are 10-100 times higher than consumer card limits, giving the owner a much greater credit capacity.

Personal credit cards are not designed to be used to grow businesses. Their limits are notably smaller because an individual doesn't require as much capacity as a business does. For example, you might need only $2,000 to purchase a really nice personal computer, but for your business, you might need $10,000 to buy multiple computers.

So, by default, limits on business cards are much greater than consumer cards. This gives the business owner the ability to get very high limit accounts and to do so within 90 days or less from starting to build their business credit.

#4 — Anyone can see your business credit

In the consumer credit world, anyone who pulls credit must have permissible purpose according to the FCRA (and so, your permission). But in the business world, anyone who wants to pull your credit can do so.

This means that your customers, clients, prospects, and even competitors can easily see what's on your credit reports. They can easily access your credit scores, payment history, high credit limits, balances on accounts, tax lien data, collection data, and so much more — all for as little as $15.

Since this information is so readily available, it is essential that business credit reports be built and maintained — because they are a reflection of you and your business.

And of course, almost all credit issuers and lenders pull business credit before making a lending decision. So, without business credit, your ability to get real corporate credit or loans is significantly reduced.

#5 — There are 3 steps to build business credit

As great as business credit is, Entrepreneur.com reports that 90% of business owners have no idea how to build it. But once the initial profile and score are built, it's then easy to continue to use the EIN credit to qualify for more and more credit.

The key is to START building business credit. Once this is done, it becomes much easier to obtain more and more credit at your heart's desire.

The first step in building business credit is to get approved for vendor accounts. These are credit issuers who will give you initial credit even if you have none now. Vendors such as Uline and Quill offer products you and your customers want and need, and they report your credit to the business bureaus — thus helping you establish initial business credit.

With five vendor accounts reported on your business credit reports, you'll have tradelines, a business score, and a profile. That will then be enough to move on to the second step of building business credit, which is getting store credit cards.

Dell, Apple, Lowes, Staples, Amazon, and most other retailers do offer business credit cards without tradelines or a personal guarantee. Some retailers, like Amazon, will approve you for credit even if you only have five reported tradelines, while others, like Home Depot, might require 10 or more. Regardless, most major retailers do offer corporate credit.

Once you have 10 reported tradelines, you can then start getting approved for cash credit cards such as Visa and MasterCard accounts that you can use anywhere. Limits are commonly between $5,000-10,000 initially, and this type of credit can be obtained within about 4-6 months from starting to build initial business credit.

Summary

Business credit provides so many benefits that it simply can't be ignored. Getting high limit accounts, getting access to credit quickly, not needing to supply a personal guarantee or a personal credit check, as well as having access to much more credit than one can ever obtain on the consumer side are only a few of these major benefits. Make sure that you introduce business credit to your customers. This way, while you are repairing their consumer credit, you can also be helping them build their EIN credit, providing even more value for your services.

For more information about building business credit and providing it as a another revenue stream, visit my podcast at **CreditRepairCloud.com/YouTub**e, as I have recorded several videos on this topic.

10 Steps To Launching Your Credit Repair Business

Starting a new business, any kind of new business, can be overwhelming. Starting a credit repair company can be even more so because a large part of your time will be consumed with learning the ins and outs of the credit system.

However, as startups go, a credit repair business is one of the most affordable startups you'll ever find. The profit potential is huge, and all you need to get started is a computer and a desire to help people. With the right focus, you can launch this business in less than 30 days.

Many people struggle with figuring out where to even begin. In our experience, here are the 10 most important details to get ironed out:

Your Company Name

This seems obvious, but your name is a crucial part of how potential customers and affiliate partners will view your business. The name should be clear, memorable, and professional. People shouldn't have to guess what your business does, but something dry like "Acme Credit Repair" will be difficult for people to remember. Try to choose something that reflects your personality and conveys a feeling of confidence.   Once you've chosen a name, do a simple online search to make sure no other credit repair companies are using that name. It is also useful to search the domain that you'd like to use (i.e., www.acmecreditrepair.com) to see if it is available before moving forward.

Your Web Site

It would be very difficult to bring on new clients without a website. After all, this is the public face of your business. Not only are websites a great source of information for potential clients, they also add legitimacy to your business. If you need a professional website fast, visit www.mycreditrepairsite.com to create a complete prewritten site in minutes with no skill required.

Once you launch your site, you can change the images, colors and text to make it unique. If you're a Credit Repair Cloud user, you can add the Web Lead Form from your Credit Repair Cloud so leads and clients can request a consultation or sign up right on your site. And if you use Chargebee, your clients can add a credit card to start their monthly payments to you. This will save you hours and headaches.

If you have the budget for it, you can hire a local web designer to build you a custom site that's clear, professional, and engaging. And if you add a lot of unique and original text to your site or even start an informative blog, Google will reward you with more traffic. When you're ready, submit your site to Google to be added to their listings. You can submit your site at www.google.com/addurl.

Credit Repair Software

It will be difficult to scale your credit repair business without credit repair software to manage it all. Credit Repair Cloud is designed to grow and scale your business. It imports credit reports, analyzes them, and creates dispute letters faster than any other method. It also improves communication with clients and affiliates, and gives you the opportunity to share valuable educational resources with clients and prospects. Best of all, it reduces your workload to less than 5 minutes per client per month. Just 2 clients can cover the cost — and all the rest is profit. So that makes it very affordable. Just remember: if you're going to spend your whole day in one software, make it one that you love.

*Tip: if you do use Credit Repair Cloud, take advantage of our free software training (it'll get you up to speed in no time).

Design Your Pricing Structure

The two most common ways credit repair businesses charge clients are "Monthly Recurring Subscription" or "Pay-Per-Delete." Here's a description of each:

Monthly recurring payments

Monthly recurring payments are the key to profits. Make a plan that is simple and affordable. Don't have dozens of plans based on what you think a certain client can pay. Think big! The goal is to have hundreds (or thousands) of people each paying you a simple monthly fee. For this to happen, it must be affordable. With credit repair software, your work will be minimal (around 5 minutes per client per month when you've got your flow down), so charge a minimal fee.

Hint: the biggest credit repair firm in the country (initials are L.L.) charges most clients between $59 and $99 a month. Successful credit repair companies make millions of dollars by all following this same simple flow:

- Charge your client an affordable low monthly fee
- Be awesome, and give awesome service so your client will continue to pay you (and refer their friends)
- Each month add new paying clients
- If you add more paying clients than you lose, your revenue will grow larger every month

A successful monthly recurring revenue business looks like this:

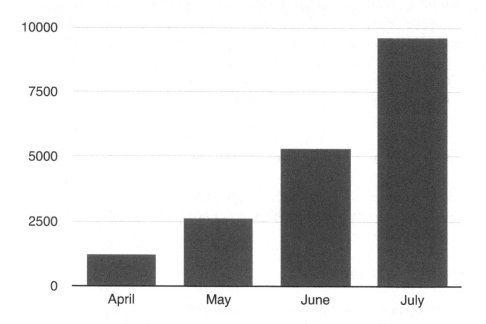

But a pay-per-delete business model always stays flat like this:

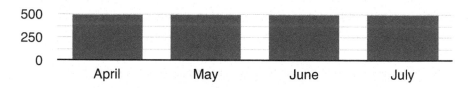

So the moral of the story is...

If you want your business to be scaleable and lasting — charge monthly rather than pay-per-delete. Pay-Per-Delete is not a good business model. It can never grow very far because you cannot scale yourself or your time, so you can never achieve critical mass. It will be a lot of work with little pay off. This the biggest and most successful credit repair companies always charge affordable monthly recurring payments.

Learn more at http://www.creditrepaircloud.com/blog/pay-per-delete-good-business-model/

Merchant Account And Gateway

This is not a requirement from the start, because you can certainly take cash and checks from clients, but if you ever want to take credit cards, you'll need a merchant account for credit repair services. This is not as easy as it sounds because most merchant account providers will not allow credit repair — because they consider it to be "high risk," which they lump in the same category as vapor cigarettes and tech support services. For that reason, you need to contact a merchant account provider who specializes in your type of business. Visit www.creditrepaircloud.com/merchant for details.

Recurring Payments Platform

If you plan on growing your business, this is a crucial element that you do not want to skip! A payment platform and a merchant gateway are not the same thing. In order to have a successful credit repair business, you will need both of them (and they must work together). A recurring payments platform is software that creates the billing plans for your clients and collects monthly recurring payments from your clients. It also sends "dunning" letters when cards decline or are about to expire. It pays for itself in the extra revenue it collects for you. Click here to see the necessary parts for automated recurring payments: www.creditrepaircloud.com/resources and download the "Guide To Getting Paid At Credit Repair."

Business Cards, Flyers, Brochures, Etc

Business cards are inexpensive to make. You can get awesome business cards for under $20 at vistaprint.com or moo.com. You can make flyers and brochures a few at a time at your local copy shop or FedEx Office. And if you're a Credit Repair Cloud user, check out the marketing art templates in the "Bonus Materials" button in your Credit Repair Cloud.

Affiliate Partners

Corporate and affiliate partners are some of the most important relationships you will need for your credit repair company to grow. Corporate partners are local businesses like law firms, CPAs, and designers that you will work with on an ongoing basis for your business needs. It is crucial to build great relationships with these types of professionals for any advice or help you will need as your business grows. Ask around in your network to see if anyone has referrals so you can start the relationship with a strong personal introduction. Affiliate partners are companies like auto dealers, mortgage brokers, and other lenders that often have to turn individuals down because their credit is poor. Making relationships with affiliate partners and showing them the mutual benefits of a relationship can be a priceless pipeline of new business. See the "Affiliates" chapter.

Making It Official

Starting at business (at home or on the side) is awesome, but at some point you need to decide on operating as a sole proprietorship/partnership, C-corporation, S-corporation, LLC, or — in some cases — non-profit. Your tax preparer or CPA will be able to tell you which one will bring you the most savings. If you're starting this business after working for someone else, you'll be shocked at the tax benefits of running our own company and in most cases, you'll be holding on to much more of your income.

Relax

Rome wasn't built in a day. Your business won't be either. Take it slow and do a little at a time. Starting a credit repair company is an exciting undertaking. However, it can be difficult to wade through the thousands of blogs, articles, and advertisements to get the information you really need to get started. By following the steps outlined here, you will be well on your way to signing your first clients.

State Regulations For A Credit Repair Business

There are countless questions that people have when considering entering the credit repair space. Many have a passion for credit repair and have started researching how to start a business, but are confused about the federal and state requirements for actually opening their doors. Requirements frequently change, so we always recommend consulting a local attorney to make sure you are compliant with all the necessary requirements. For details, visit www.creditrepaircloud.com/all-states.

There are three primary types of state requirements that credit repair companies may need to get started:

Surety Bond: A Surety Bond is an agreement that protects individuals who engage with a Credit Services Organization from possible monetary damages that could occur from the relationship. This primarily applies to credit repair companies who charge clients for their services up front. When you use a bond service, You'd typically need to pay just 2-3% of the total bond amount (depending on your credit score).. For questions about Bonds and to see if one is required for your state, visit www.Surety1.com and www.BondsExpress.com or contact your local insurance agent. Shop around and compare prices.

Business License: Generally, a business license is a permit issued by your city, as a requirement to open any type of business. A business license is very affordable. For many cities, it's under $100. At the time of this writing, only _one_ state (Idaho) requires credit repair companies to be licensed.

Incorporation: Incorporation is generally not a requirement, but you may choose to incorporate for tax reasons. When deciding where to establish your credit repair company, it is important to remember that you have to incorporate your business in the same state where it is physically located.

Which States Are The Most Difficult?

We have categorized all US states into five difficulty groups based on the amount and severity of state regulations. Keep in mind that this refers only to state regulations — there are always federal regulations that all US credit repair companies must comply with.

Very Easy: In these states, there are no state regulations for credit repair companies: Alabama, Alaska, Montana, New Jersey, New Mexico, North Dakota, Rhode Island South Dakota, Vermont and Wyoming.

Easy: In these states there are some state regulations, but no real registration requirements (there may be surety bond requirements): Arizona, Arkansas, Connecticut, Florida, Illinois, Indiana, Maine, Massachusetts, Michigan, New Hampshire, New York, North Carolina, and Pennsylvania.

Moderate: The majority of states have some additional registration or bond requirements, but they are easy to meet: California, Delaware, Hawaii, Idaho, Iowa, Kansas, Kentucky, Minnesota, Mississippi, Missouri, Nebraska, Nevada, Ohio, Oklahoma, Oregon, Tennessee, Texas, Utah, Virginia, Washington, West Virginia, and Wisconsin.

Difficult: A few states have stricter registration and bonding requirements, and may require an annual registration fee: Colorado, Louisiana, Maryland, and South Carolina.

Very Difficult: In Georgia, a credit repair company MUST be a 501(c)(3) non-profit organization or an attorney. It is a misdemeanor to operate as a credit repair company in Georgia without fulfilling these requirements.

Specific costs, requirements, and paperwork can be found on your state government's website. It is important to make sure you are complying with all necessary state and federal regulations when you start your credit repair company. Rules do vary from state to state, if you have questions about regulations in your state, please consult an attorney.

For more information like this, visit www.creditrepaircloud.com/all-states.

Checklist For Starting A Credit Repair Business

Starting a new business may seem overwhelming, but once you break it down into small, achievable goals, it becomes very easy to accomplish.

☐ **Credit Repair Software**
Software saves you time by automating most of the work. It also keeps you organized, gives a professional face to your business, and helps you scale quickly. The best software of course is Credit Repair Cloud which you can try for free at CreditRepairCloud.com.

☐ **Credit Repair Training and Certificate**
Credit repair education for you and your staff gives you the expertise and credibility to really solve your clients' credit issues. It also gives you an awesome certificate to place on your wall. Sign up at www.americancreditrepairacademy.com.

☐ **Business Web Site**
A professional website goes a long way towards giving your business credibility. Get one in minutes at www.mycreditrepairsite.com. Paid Credit Repair Cloud users get a coupon code for two free months of web hosting (Check your upgrade letter).

☐ **Merchant Account and Gateway**
Getting paid is easier when you're able to accept credit card payments from clients. For this, you must have a merchant account and gateway that will allow for credit repair charges. Most merchant accounts and gateways will not allow this, so find one that will at www.creditrepaircloud.com/merchant.

☐ **Recurring Payments Software**
A recurring payment software It makes collecting automated recurring monthly payments much easier. It's "dunning" service continues to try cards that fail. It's an awesome value and it is nearly impossible to grow a successful recurring revenue credit repair business without this. Learn more https://www.creditrepaircloud.com/guide-to-getting-paid.

☐ **Business Cards and Brochures**
Credit repair is a people business, so business cards and brochures help you make an impression. We have some basic templates to get you stated. Credit Repair Cloud users will find them in the Bonus Materials of their account. For getting them printed, we love vistaprint.com and moo.com (or just visit your local copy shop)

☐ **Client Agreement**
See the Client Intake Docs chapter for a detailed discussion. Credit Repair Cloud users already have this built-in.

☐ **Fees**
Most companies charge between $59 and $99 a month. This all depends on your clientele. Decide on your fees and be consistent with them. However, you may want to give a discount to a couple.

☐ **A Client Signup Form On Your Site**
Manual ways to add new signups into your client database are rather tedious. If you're a Credit Repair Cloud user, the web lead form code in your Credit Repair Cloud (under My Company>Web Site Tools) creates a form that automatically sends leads and signups right to your Credit Repair Cloud.

☐ **Toll Free Number (Optional)**
Need a Toll-Free 800 number, Virtual PBX, virtual fax or email call notifications? We use Kall8 ourselves and we love them. Learn more at http://www.toll-free800.com/15478.htm.

☐ **Working Voicemail**
Whatever you are doing right now, stop and set up your voicemail. You must have a working voicemail to run a business (and make sure it's not full)! With each client easily having a potential revenue of $1,000 or more, missed calls become costly.

☐ **Professional Email**
Do not run a business on Yahoo, Hotmail, or AOL email. These are not professional or reliable. Set up an email address with your own

domain (or at least use Gmail). Not only is Gmail free, but it's accepted as professional.

☐ **Have Employees Sign an NDA With A Non-Compete Clause**
Credit repair is a great business. But you don't want your employees to steal all of your ideas and become your competition, right? If you're a Credit Repair Cloud user, you will find the NDA form in your Bonus Materials (on the home page after login).

☐ **Check for any Special State Requirements**
We make awesome software to run your business, but we can't give legal advice — so check with your attorney (or your state) for any special requirements to do business in your state. See www.creditrepaircloud.com/all-states.

Got questions: We're here to help! Visit **www.CreditRepairCloud.com** and click "Contact Us."

Working With Clients

Get Your Clients To Love You (And Make More Money)

A savvy business owner in any industry knows that a client relationship can live long beyond the initial sale. This is especially true in the credit repair industry. It is easy to see a credit repair client as a one-off relationship: you approach a lead, convert him into a client, work with him to improve his credit report, then end the relationship when the job is done. However, by effectively managing the relationship, you can help that client with ancillary services, gain referrals, improve your advertising, and improve business partnerships. Below are some crucial tips to keep in mind to get the most out of your client relationships.

1. Success begins with the first contact: In your initial conversation with a prospect, keep in mind that you are building a relationship with a lifetime partner, not a single sale. Ask about their overall financial situation and what they hope to achieve in the future. Don't just talk about your services; learn about their goals. Show integrity and be truthful. Don't promise anything you cannot deliver on.

2. Focus on building a relationship, not selling services: By truly listening and understanding a person's credit and financial situation, opportunities for cross-monetization or up-selling will happen organically. Once you have succeeded in helping to repair the

customer's credit report, you will easily be aware of what other financial services he might benefit from. This is also a great opportunity to build relationships with affiliate partners, as you may be able to refer the customer to them. As with any relationship, the benefits should be mutual. A customer should always leave a conversation feeling like they are being taken care of, even if it is also benefitting your business.

3. It's the little things: Make sure that your customers know they are not just another number. Small gestures can make customers feel supported and cared for. Send a birthday card, thank you note, or beneficial information on credit or finance that you think might benefit them.

4. Use marketing automation to strengthen client relationships: High quality marketing automation can be used to manage client relationships you're your client volume is too high for regular contact. This automation can be sequenced to provide regular updated or education to clients without spending time contacting each person individually. Automated emails should feel personal and include quality information.

5. Provide value: In order to build a lasting relationship, clients should see you as an expert in your field, not just a one-time service provider. Accomplish this by providing educational materials on the credit industry and beyond. Regularly educate your clients on how to holistically improve their financial standing. By doing so, clients will begin to see you as someone they can trust and come to you for information on other services.

6. Create an official referral program: When you have successfully provided a quality service, be sure to ask clients if there is anyone else in their personal or professional network who may benefit from your services. If a referral comes through, make sure to follow up with the original client to thank them. Provide a benefit for the referral, whether it be a free service, discount, or simply a handwritten thank you card.

7. Collect testimonials: Always keep track of your successes and share them with clients and prospects with testimonials. This can be as simple as a few written sentences, a voicemail recording from a

satisfied client, or a cell phone video. One of the best ways to market your services is with legitimate customer testimonials. There is never a better time to get them than immediately after a success.

By following these steps and creating quality, mutually beneficial relationship with clients, you can grow your business with strengthened affiliate partnerships, better quality advertising, and a growing base of referrals. Customers are more likely to continue to work with professionals that they trust and respect, so remember that building relationships is the key to success.

Always Be Transparent With Your Clients

Always make sure your client is involved in determining what you're disputing for them and why and never hide the work you're doing or the letters you're sending for them. Remember, the dispute letters are coming from the client, so this is a time for total transparency. Plus, disputing something without the client's awareness can get you into serious legal trouble.

Give 'Em The Pickle!

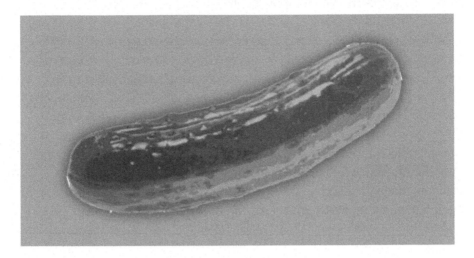

Your existing customers are your greatest asset. Keeping them happy will increase your revenue and profitability. If you have 2 minutes, go to youtube right now and watch this awesome video of great and simple advice for anyone with customers. https://www.youtube.com/watch?v=ISJ1V8vBiiI

*If you have trouble with that link, see our blog at CreditRepairCloud.com/blog or search YouTube for "Give 'Em the Pickle by Bob Farrell - Customer Service." You must see this awesome five minute video. It will change your business.

Accessing Client's Credit Reports

One of the questions we hear most often from people who are considering starting their own credit repair company is "How do I access credit reports for my clients?" Historically, there is no easy response to this question. Mortgage brokers, car dealerships and other lenders have the ability to pull credit reports directly from credit bureaus. However, bureaus will not allow credit repair companies to pull client credit reports directly. Most credit repair companies have their clients signup for a credit monitoring free trial. After that free trial has ended, there are several different price options for clients, ranging from $19.95 to $29.95 per month, depending on the company. This fee is paid directly by clients. Many of the report providers will even pay you a commission if you become their affiliate. Check your Credit Repair Cloud account under MY COMPANY>CREDIT MONITORING SERVICE for details.

The most successful credit repair companies are those that have a smooth process for accessing credit reports and importing them into the software. By working with a software like Credit Repair Cloud, you will able to convert more clients, scale your business, and allow your sales representatives to focus on finding new clients, rather than tracking down credit reports.

Importing Credit Reports

Credit Repair Cloud uses technology to import the clients reports and scores into the software, saving hours of typing. The software automatically analyzes the report and flags the problem areas. Each month thereafter, if the client keeps the credit monitoring subscription, the new reports and scores are imported into the software where it tracks all the changes. In many ways, accessing client credit reports is the Achilles' heel of the credit repair industry. Thats why having a good smooth solution like we have with our "Client Onboarding" can make a big difference in the growth of your customer base. It automatically guides your clients through the process, and they can even do it from their smartphone.

Start By Listening

In your role as an advisor to your credit repair client, you'll find that your business is one part logic and one part emotion. Most clients come to you with a specific need or goal in mind. Sometimes it's a home purchase or a small business loan, maybe just an overall cleanup. Either way, there is usually a life story or situation that caused the credit issue.

When working with people, always ask questions that let them to know that you recognize their struggle. It is so easy to get wrapped up talking about creditors, collections, payment history & disputes. But, many times, you need to take a moment and let your clients talk. Allow them time to "say what they need to say." Credit repair requires you to be that coach and counselor who listens and lets them know that it will be okay. Emotional support is key to a successful credit repair practice.

I have experienced the greatest joy by helping clients. It is a wonderful feeling when you receive a "thank you" card in the mail with a picture of your client's new home, or that fantastic referral you get from a recent success story. The logical credit repair strategy (the game plan) is supported by a client who is motivated to succeed and emotionally attached to a goal. This is no different from your goal of being a successful credit repair professional.

Remember: if you give awesome service, your clients will continue to pay your monthly fee. They'll refer their friends, and that is how you grow your business. Keep in mind that they see you as an expert and make time to learn your craft.

Credit repair is a fantastic niche that really helps people get the things they need and want for themselves and their family. What a fantastic way to make a living: helping people.

3 Questions For New Clients

3 QUESTIONS FOR NEW CLIENTS

Let's be frank: there is no "one size fits all" solution for credit repair. The nature of providing credit repair services is that each client you work with will be a completely unique case. It is crucial to spend time speaking to each client to understand their current credit situation and their credit goals. This is important, not only to inform the basic repair process, but also because it provides an opportunity to offer additional services that translate to more money for your business.

For example, let's say you are approached by a professional hoping to repair her credit so she can buy a home. After reviewing her credit report, you determine that there are three to four inaccurate or unverifiable items that can be disputed. If you provide only this basic service, this relationship would earn your company less than $1,000 and may not solve the client's entire problem. Alternatively, you could spend some time delving further into the client's goals to see if there are additional services that might benefit her. These types of qualification methods cannot only create additional revenue streams, but also position you as a trusted expert to your client base.

There are three basic questions that you can ask a new client to determine what types of services would best benefit him/her:

1. **What made you contact me today?**

   This is usually the first question we recommend asking a client or potential client. It will help you to get a sense of their goals, timelines, and pain points. Most people don't know much about credit repair. Your job is to listen to their problems and tell them the best plan of action, even if it is not what they originally thought they needed. A client might think that he or she only needs some basic disputing assistance, but after further discussions realizes that he or she should actually pursue a lawsuit against a credit bureau for violating the Fair Credit Reporting Act (FCRA). By listening to a client's answer to this basic question, you can begin to drill down to what their actual problem is and how to most effectively solve it.

2. **Why now?**

   Most people will only seek out your services at a breaking point. A client may contact you to repair their credit because he or she is tired of having collections agencies threatening their income. As a credit repair professional, you will be able to offer not only to repair his or her credit, but also provide advice on responding to violations to the Fair Debt Collection Practices Act (FDCPA). Identifying the breaking point will give you an idea of whether there is more than one problem that needs to be solved.

3. **Are you a small business owner?**

   The number of small business owners in the US has increased 49% since 1982. A client may approach you to repair his or her individual credit, without knowing that you are also able to provide business credit services. Asking this basic question can help create a rich revenue stream and provide a great benefit to your client.

As a credit repair professional, it is important to think of yourself as an advisor rather than just a service provider. You know the industry much better than you clients do, so it is up to you to help them determine what services will benefit them the most. Ask good questions and really listen to their responses. Getting comfortable with this practice will allow you to provide the best service possible to your clients while creating additional revenue streams for your business.

Then as soon as possible, get the potential client to sign up for $1 trial of credit monitoring (at a compatible report provider) so it will import into Credit Repair Cloud

Next, you run Simple Audit with 1 click, to create an awesome credit analysis report that will guide you and your client through the rest of the free consultation. It help to close the sale by highlighting the benefits of working with you.

Getting Started With Your First Client

So, you advertise your credit repair service, you set up a site, you set up a client portal, you visit Mortgage Brokers and Real Estate Agents and ask for referrals. Finally, clients call and you schedule an appointment with them. When you meet with a new client, you should explain the credit repair process.

The Simple Audit Report is your greatest sales tool

If they only want to just have a free consultation, wow them by importing their reports, then click "Save as pending and run Simple Audit" to show your potential client an awesome custom credit analysis report outlining the issues, and clear recommendations showing the value and benefit of your services. Use that Simple Audit report to guide your consultation.

If the want to sign up and be your client, awesome! Complete their client profile in Credit Repair Cloud, set an agreement, turn portal access on, and instruct them to log in sign your agreement and complete the onboarding process, so you'll be ready to get started on their accounts.

*These items are given to the client at the start of service:
- Fee Agreement Contract (Explains your fees)
- Consumer Credit File Rights (Explains their legal rights)
- Fair Debt Practices Act (Explains their rights)
- Authorization for Credit Repair Action (or Power of Attorney Letter)
- Also be sure to explain your fees during your first contact.

*If you're using Credit Repair Cloud, these items are already in the default agreement that a client signs the first time they log into your portal.

Make sure your clients understand that they will need to sign up for a $1 trial to a credit monitoring service to see monthly changes to their reports and scores. They will sign up for these themselves and pay the monthly fee. You can even choose a report provider who will pay you an affiliate commission. See the chapter about ordering reports and the list of providers in Credit Repair Cloud (under MY COMPANY>CREDIT MONITORING SERVICE).

After you've imported the report, saved it as pending and run Simple Audit, your next step is to tag and save the pending report. To do this, return to the pending report. This is where you go through the entire report onscreen with the client. Credit Repair Cloud will have already flagged and highlighted the negative items in red, so all you do is go through the list, while you talk over each item with your client. You'll scroll down the list and choose an "reason" and an "instruction" for each item (don't worry you can change those choices later if you make a mistake). The important part is to complete this process for each negative item on the page. Next, click "save" at the bottom, and you've just planned out the entire lifecycle of this client. Congratulations!

Now you're ready to start to create the first round of letters, for a handful of those items, and you'll do that in Dispute Wizard 3. Not sure how any of this works? No worries, there are videos in the top of every page of the software, to walk you through each step. And if you need some extra help, click in the software to schedule a call with us. We'll assist you personally.

Pro Tip About Billing

I have seen thousands of credit repair companies launch grow, flourish or fail. The companies that do the best follow the other leaders in this business.

- Many states don't allow you to charge up front for credit repair. So instead, many companies will charge a "First Work" fee near the beginning, after they've done some work and created the round 1 letters.

- 30 days later, they charge a small monthly fee (recurring each month).

If you're using Credit Repair Cloud, and have your processes down, your work will be reduced to *less than five minutes per month* per client. So a small fee is more than appropriate. The goal isn't to gouge the clients and take their money, the goal is to have as many happy clients as you can, all paying your small affordable monthly fee.

The client should discuss the items on the report with you, as you tag and save the items from the report into the software. Together you will come up with the game plan. Manage their expectations by letting them know that this is a process and that will only be disputing just a few items per month and that it takes 30 days to see changes start to happen. Start with the obvious errors first and you will always look like hero when they come off fast. Then concentrate on the items within the most recent 24 months, as those carry the most weight on the score. Wait for the results to come back, you'll either have a win, or you may need to challenge the results. Remember "if they can't prove it, they most remove it." Repeat the process if necessary. Lather, rinse, repeat.

Pro Tip: Want more sales? Offer new clients a money back guarantee if they are not satisfied! If you're giving awesome service, only 1% will ever take you up on that offer, but having that offer will multiply your number of signups.

Educate Your Clients

Cleaning up credit reports is awesome, but an equally important part of your job is to educate your clients so they wont fall back into the same bad patterns that got them into credit trouble in the first place. If your client continues to apply for credit, if they pay any bills late, or if they continue to max out their credit cards — guess what? Their score will suffer.

7 important tips to pass onto your clients:

- **Don't apply for credit.** Each time you do, your score suffers a hit.

- **Don't co-sign.** When you co-sign on someone else's loan, you're agreeing to be responsible for it. If that person doesn't pay the bill, your credit score suffers.

- **Pay your bills on time.** One past due payment can decrease your score by *100 points*. Ouch! If you've accidentally missed a payment call the credit card company immediately. If you're a good customer, they will often wave a past-due posting if you ask.

- **Pay credit card balances down to less than 25% of the available credit line.** If your credit line is $10,000, never use more than $2,500. Never max out your credit cards, even if you pay them off each month. This quick trick will boost your score.

- **Monitor your credit with a credit monitoring service.** You can find a current list of reports that will import in the Credit Repair Cloud software.

- **Don't over-promise on rapid results, rapid score increases, or anything that is not true.** Explain to them that bureaus are slow. Scores don't change overnight and the creditors don't report changes to the bureaus immediately. It all takes time.

- **Your clients must forward to you ALL correspondence they receive from the dispute letters that you send.** Without this you are working blind. Credit Monitoring will not show you what is in the letters. Your clients must forward them to you or you cannot do your job. So when you've set a reminder to follow up on a dispute item, also check to see if your client has forwarded the response letter they've received.

Financial Tools For Your Clients

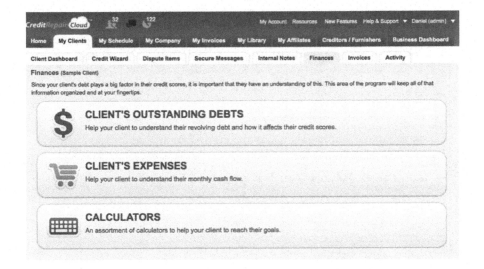

If you're a Credit Repair Cloud user, encourage your clients to use the financial tools in their Client Portal. They can monitor available credit, debts, expenses, and more with the "Finances" tab in their Client Login Portal. You have these same tools in each client account in your Credit Repair Cloud.

These calculators are in your clients account in your Credit Repair Cloud. They are also in every client's portal. Use them. For example, the available-credit ratio really works. That one trick will usually increase a score dramatically.

How does this generate more revenue?

Because you're in a "service" business. Going the extra mile to help educate clients will increase customer satisfaction. Happy clients will stay longer, which increases their average lifetime value. Their positive word of mouth will bring you more referrals and more money. So there's no doubt about it: taking time to educate your clients will put extra money in your pocket. *Cha-ching!*

CLIENT'S DEBTS (Sample Client)

CLIENT'S DEBTS

If your client carries high credit card (revolving) debt, they should be aware of what their finance (APR) charges are for each account and you might want to suggest that they focus on paying down the accounts with the highest interest (APR) rate first. This will save them the most money.

A higher FICO score will qualify your client for a lower interest rate (APR). Maxing out credit cards looks bad to the Credit Bureaus and lowers a credit score. If your clients carry high credit card balances, here is a trick that will often boost a score considerably (and quickly); Instruct the client to pay all of their credit cards down to where the balance owed (B2AC) is below 25-30% of the available limit.

In this form on the right, enter the client's account balances, credit limits and APR interest rates. It will calculate their total debt and "balance-to-available-limit" (B2AC) ratio, to show what they need to focus on for maximum results.

To maximize a score, instruct your client to keep their "balance-to-available-limit" ratio below 25-30%.

Available Credit Limit, 79.95%

Good, 25%

Current Balance, 19.96

CLIENT'S CREDIT ACCOUNTS

For | July | 2014 | **Submit**

Account/Card	APR	Limit	Balance	Ratio	
AMEX	9	10000	2500	25	%
Visa	8	10000	2500	25	%
Mastercard	12	12000	3000	25	%
	0	0	0	0	%
	0	0	0	0	%
	0	0	0	0	%
	0	0	0	0	%
	0	0	0	0	%
	0	0	0	0	%
	0	0	0	0	%
	0	0	0	0	%
	0	0	0	0	%
	0	0	0	0	%
		32000	8000	25	%

* B2AC = Balance to Available Credit   Limit   Balance   Ratio   %

Delete   **Update**   **Print**

Top 5 Ways To Give Awesome Customer Service!

If you're starting a credit repair business, customer service is the one element that can make or break you, because you are in a people business. We have developed this list to help you provide your customers with phenomenal customer support! This way, they will continue to pay your monthly fee — and will also tell everyone they know how great you are! We hope this helps you in building your business!

Tip 1 - Build a relationship

Sure, you're doing business, but people love to interact with someone that is personable. Create a relationship with your client. A good way that I have found is when you are talking to a customer and they mention their dog, kids, or something important to them — you make a note of it. The Credit Repair Cloud has a great memo/note section that your staff can utilize. In a month or so, when you follow up with that client, mention their pet or kids, or wish them Happy Birthday. They will love that you remembered who they were and that they weren't just another transaction to you.

Tip 2 - Go the extra mile

Go above and beyond to make sure your clients know that you appreciate their business! Send them a handwritten birthday card or a thank you. It's simple things like this that allow your customers to rave to everyone they know about why your company is the best!

Tip 3 - Listen

When your client calls about something silly, give them your undivided attention. Although the issue may seem tedious to you, it may have caused them great frustration. Hear their issues and relate to them. Simple enough. Remember that the most important part of the job is to educate your clients on how to better manage their credit and their finances so they can maintain their awesome credit long after your work is done.

Tip 4 - Positive attitude

A positive attitude goes a long way in customer service! They want to know you are excited to help them! Your tone and attitude will make or break how customers respond to you. After all, it's difficult to be mean to someone who is nice and wanting to help you.

Tip 5 - Remember why you're in business

Let's face it: if there were no customers, you wouldn't have a job. It is as simple as that. Therefore, you have to keep them happy and be sure that you are providing them with good customer service at all costs. This means you need to answer their questions, help them in finding what they need, solve their problems, and meet their demands *in a quick and professional fashion.*

*Be sure to see the Pickle Video mentioned in the "Give 'em the pickle!" chapter. It's a life changer.

How To Improve Credit Scores Using Personal Loans

When advising your credit repair clients on improving their FICO scores, one tool you can suggest is taking out a personal loan. Personal loans are offered by most banks and are relatively easy to get. Many banks are offering up to $100,000 for people with high incomes and good credit. Personal loans can be used for a variety of purposes, one of which is to rapidly raise a FICO score — by using the lion share to pay off credit card debt.

Taking out a personal loan to pay off credit card debt can have the dual benefit of eliminating accounts with balances while also reducing the credit card utilization rate. Doing so could result in FICO score growth in the 100s within a month.

Paying off one debt with another debt may seem counterintuitive, but the real benefit to a client's FICO score is the transition from *revolving debt* to *installment debt*. The "debt utilization ratio" on the FICO score only includes credit card debt, not installment debt. Therefore, even though the client will have the same amount of debt, their debt utilization ratio will decrease, as will their outstanding balances. Additionally, some personal loans have lower interest rates than many credit cards, which won't affect the credit score but may help the client pay the debt off faster. It can be helpful to further advise that they do not close out credit cards with no balance, as these can help their credit scores.

As your credit repair company continues to grow, so will your credit toolbox. Using personal loans to pay off credit card debt is one of many pieces of advice you can offer to clients to improve their credit scores and help them reach their goals.

Buying Or Selling "Trade Lines"

People ask us about this all the time. As a rule of thumb, if it sounds too good to be true, it is. Don't fall for scammy spammy things that are not legal. If you encourage your client to buy trade lines (placement on credit lines that belong to strangers) to help them to qualify for a mortgage, that client can go to prison for mortgage fraud (a federal offense). If you're getting added to a family member's card, thats a different solution called "piggybacking" which is perfectly acceptable, but if you're buying or selling "trade-lines" you may want to rethink your business so you won't end up in the pokey. It's not worth it. Let's help people and not hurt them.

How Many Credit Cards Should A Client Have?

I hear a lot of advice from friends, experts, and strangers on how many credit cards one should have to achieve the optimal credit score. One friend told me that seven credit cards was ideal, another "read somewhere" that the ideal number was three. After the great recession, experts all advised against the evil of credit cards. With all the conjecture, how many credit cards should you advise your clients to keep?

The easy answer to this question is: it doesn't matter. Most people have several lines of credit on their credit scores, including retail, general, gas, etc. One person may have 15 credit cards open with almost no revolving debt; another might only have two but they have high balances and frequent late payments. In this case, the number of cards isn't very important — the balance and payment history is, so keeping old accounts open, rather than closing them, will generally work in your favor.

Credit card haters often say that having too many lines of debt is bad for your credit. This is untrue. As long as the consumer pays all cards on time and doesn't have a high usage rate, the number of cards doesn't matter. Additionally, the old wives' tale that consumers have to use all open credit cards each month or they will hurt their credit is false. The important thing is to pay all credit cards on time and to not have a high balance of revolving debt (try to keep it below 30% of the total credit line). Don't pay much attention to all the conjecture about how many credit cards are necessary: as long as clients maintain their payments, don't get in over their heads, their scores will be great!

The Best Way To Grow Your Business

Always Be Awesome!

As simple as it sounds, this is the best way to grow your business.

Let's think as a consumer. When you love a product or service, you'll rave about it with your family and friends. This is the best advertising there is and it will grow your business like wildfire.

Yes, you can take out ads and pay affiliates to refer clients and do all the standard things folks do to grow a business. But when you start to deliver an awesome service that people really rave about, that's when you begin to grow exponentially. No money can buy that kind of advertising.

Want to have success beyond your wildest dreams? Be *awesome*.

5 Ways To Be Truly Awesome With Your Credit Repair Business

1. **Be the "trusted expert" to your clients and your affiliates**

   Educate them. This is going to be 90% of what you do. Help them set budgets and understand their finances. Use the tools and resources in the client portal for this. Be a teacher.

2. **Give amazing service**

   The fact is, clients don't understand how things work, and they want someone to do their chores for them. So do them. Help them understand how credit works. Mail letters for them. Remind them every month to forward dispute responses to you.

3. **Don't over-promise things you can't deliver**

   Be truthful in everything you do and don't make your focus about the score. Explain to them that it's a slow process. Never promise huge score jumps or that you can make a bankruptcy disappear. This will only make people very angry at you. Most credit reports have errors, so go over those first. Have the client pay down credit cards and stop applying for credit — that will increase the score. Then, dispute a few items each month. Some you'll win some you wont, but between credit education and clean up — you will improve that client's situation.

4. **Be transparent**

   Let your clients see everything you are doing. Credit repair isn't about secrets. It's something anyone can do. Share everything with them. Be an open book. Use all the capabilities in the Client Portal to allow your client to see everything you do. Our software makes it easy, and they will love you for it.

5. **Listen to your clients**

They must dictate what gets disputed and why. Involve your clients in the process. Gone are the days of sending secret letters on behalf of your clients and not letting them know what you're saying on their behalf. That will only get you into trouble!

Tips And Warnings

- The best way to make money is by ensuring that your client is happy. The rest will simply fall into place.

- To kick start your credit repair business, offer your services for a discounted price for a limited period; ensure that you do an outstanding job for those who opted for the introductory offer.

- Never be greedy with the fees.

- Never promise too much.

- Never do anything that you even suspect may be illegal, however tempting and profitable that may seem to be.

Have A Money Back Guarantee

As a credit repair specialist, you cannot guarantee that all of your client's negative items will magically vanish from their report, so it's important to explain this clearly to your clients and to offer them a money back guarantee. Many newbies just starting are terrified at the thought of giving refunds. If that's you, relax and have an open mind, and you'll see how this idea is beneficial to the well-being of your business.

We asked Roger Chlowitz, Director of Business Development at Payment Cloud—one of the biggest provider of merchant accounts for credit repair companies—for his expert perspective on money back guarantees. Here's what he had to say:

> *"We recommend that credit repair companies always have a refund policy. It's way better to offer a money back guarantee than get chargebacks, which will cost you your merchant account."*

— *Roger Chlowitz*

Here are the top 3 reasons why your credit repair business needs a money back guarantee:

1. **Promoting a money back guarantee will bring you more signups and greatly increase your revenue.**

   With a Money Back Guarantee, potential clients will feel more comfortable to sign up for your service. Because they feel comfortable at having no risk, they are far more likely to sign up. This is how you grow and scale your business (and your client list) faster.

2. **An angry client will get their money back anyway.**

   An angry customer can file a complaint at their credit card company with one phone call (or one click). This is called a chargeback. When a chargeback is filed, the customer's bank takes the money from you and gives it back to the client. It doesn't matter if you've had them sign an agreement or a charge authorization. All they need to do is say a few magic words to their bank, like "This was not authorized" or even worse "The product was damaged and not as described." When you receive a chargeback, that money gets taken from you without notice and your payment gateway charges you a fine (ouch)! And even worse, if you get too many chargebacks, you will lose your merchant account and be out of business. In a chargeback situation, your client will always win, so it's far better (and less costly) to just give a refund rather than argue with them.

3. **Refunds save time, remove stress, and improve your reputation.**

   Most "normal" people will never ask for a refund, but there are those one-off, pain-in-the-butt customers who are just looking for trouble and it's always best to just give a refund them immediately so they go away peacefully without bashing your business or filing a chargeback with their credit card company. Sure it's painful, especially if you're a new business, but the good will you create will come back to you 1000%. Your reputation is everything (and so is protecting your merchant account).

You're not alone. Bad customers and chargebacks happen to _every_ business. My friend is the manager of a fancy hotel in Bel Air, California, the elite area that's next to Beverly Hills (but much fancier). His hotel caters to movie stars and billionaires. One day we began to talk about Chargebacks and I was shocked to hear that he gets them, too!

Hotel guests will file chargebacks for their hotel room charges and for their lobster meals in the restaurant, giving them a free vacation. But before you start to get ideas that this is how to live like a king for free, remember that there is also the rule of Karma. (i.e., If you do bad things, then bad things will happen to you — but if you're good and nice, the universe will always reward you).

The good news is, having a money back guarantee and a refund policy are good and important for your business, your merchant account...and goodwill. If you take care of your clients, communicate well and try your best to give awesome service, your business will grow and your chargebacks and refunds will be under 1%.

When a client asks for their money back, don't take it personally. Give it to them immediately, wish them well, shake it off, take a deep breath and focus back on growing your business and being awesome!

Marketing

How To Promote And Market Your Credit Repair Business

Now that you have everything in place, it's time to start promoting and marketing your credit consulting business.

Call other local credit repair businesses to get an idea of the services they offer and the types of fees associated with these services. In our own PRO software we give a breakdown of suggested fees. Some credit repair specialists don't charge fees at all. For mortgage brokers and auto dealers the reward can be greater in generating leads and closing more loans. Go through all the information you can find, decide on your fees and services, and get ready to advertise.

Dress professionally and meet with local merchants who deal with financing: mortgage brokers, real estate agents, auto dealers, etc. If you've signed up for a Client Portal account and have a website, this will be a plus. Many mortgage and real estate professionals will require you to have a site before referring clients to you.

Create flyers, brochures, and business cards. Give a brief description about your services and contact information. We already provide these in the Credit-Aid Pro Bonus materials. Post flyers everywhere you can. You may also want to place small ads for your services in local newspapers, church newsletters, and periodicals.

Offer friends and family your credit repair counseling services for free, and then ask them for a letter of recommendation. This will quickly help build your client base. Word of mouth is the very best kind of advertising.

You may want to consider giving credit repair and debt seminars or classes to teach people how to help themselves. Give talks at high schools and colleges about ways to stay out of debt. The students will go home with the information you have given them, plus your business card or brochure and tell their parents, who could end up as your next clients.

Mini billboards. These are great to be seen every day by the drivers passing by, but traditional billboards can be very expensive. However, we are also starting to see small portable billboards on the side of the road. These are a nice, affordable alternative.

Magnetic sign on the side of your car. These really work! Everywhere you go, people will see this — and you can't beat the price!

Flyers and brochures. These are also excellent, affordable ways to advertise your business. You might try hanging them in restaurant and shop windows, grocery stores, laundromats, a local college, on light poles, bulletin boards, etc. Make sure you are aware of the laws in your city and that you are not violating them by placing your marketing material where it is not allowed. Also consider offering your marketing materials to referral partners like accountants, auto dealers bankers, financial planners, mortgage brokers, real estate agents, etc. Their clients are in need of your business. Some credit repair companies pay for these referrals.

Local newspaper ads, shopping guides. Newspaper ads can be very affordable. As with all marketing, your job is simply to get your services in front of as many people that need them as possible.

Internet ads, Craigslist ads, YouTube, your own web site. You can't beat free advertising!

Direct mail marketing. This can become costly and difficult to track, so test in small quantities first. Create 5-10 possible direct mail pieces and then try sending them out in groups of 200. Evaluate the productivity by assigning different website addresses. Be creative! Think about where your customers would be, what they would be reading, looking at, etc., and then place your services in front of them.

Promote your credit repair business vigorously. Advertise and offer bonuses to raise awareness of your business — such as free counseling, free consultations, free credit report assessment, lotteries, quality information and resources, and so on. It's not difficult to establish your credit repair business and make money, provided you keep the interest of your client as the most important aspect of the business. Always start with someone close: friends, family, and colleagues. That will get the word of mouth rolling. Go out of your way to do an exceptional job! Your good work will be rewarded by word-of-mouth promotion and endless leads.

To kick start your credit repair business, offer a limited time discount. And make sure to give your best effort, so those that take you up on your offer will send you more business through referrals.

Start small and work out the kinks before you expand too quickly. As a credit consultant, you should start building your business locally before expanding too fast or going to the Internet. If you build your credibility early, when you branch out, you will have experience and a history of customer satisfaction to back you up.

Stay honest with your clients. You are providing them with a very important service. They must trust you and your business. Credit repair can be confusing to many. Reassure and give them the information they want. This will enhance your credibility and increase your credit repair business well into the future.

Networking

The financial industry is big, and there is a lot of money to be made. By networking and partnering up with others in different segments of the financial industry, you can increase your bottom line and make more money. For instance, you can network with mortgage lenders, financial advisors, accountants, real estate agents, and even car salesmen — and refer business to one another. It is a win-win since everyone is in different segments of the financial industry, so there aren't any overlapping interests.

Know How To Market Yourself Online

Although there is a lot of money to be made in credit repair, it is also extremely competitive. As such, you should gain the upper edge by learning how to market yourself on the Internet. Your clients are everywhere online, be it Google, Twitter, Facebook, or LinkedIn. So the bigger digital presence you establish for yourself, the more money you will make. At the very minimum, you should have a Facebook page solely dedicated to your business and start looking for business within your Facebook network. Once you have that down, you can move onto other methods of getting business online, such as PPC marketing or search engine optimization.

Credit Repair Cloud users: Be sure to download the Marketing Art templates in your Bonus materials (on the home page after login). They are artwork for professionally designed marketing materials to customize to make your own.

How To Use Customer Testimonials

One of the most important pieces of marketing for credit repair companies is social proof. Most potential clients do not know much about credit repair and will want to make sure that you are a trusted expert in your field. With all the information available on the Internet these days, the vast majority of people will research your company before engaging in a relationship. Testimonials are one of the best ways to establish this social proof and to show prospects that you can be trusted. Unfortunately, many credit repair companies use testimonials inefficiently. Below are some of the most common testimonial questions we hear from new credit repair companies.

"I don't have any testimonials yet, should I make some up?"

No! This is a very common tactic that new companies use. It is understandable that you would want to invent testimonials until you have legitimate ones to replace them. However, these are often obviously made up and make your company seem untrustworthy. There are several things that you can use in their place until you are able to gather customer testimonials:

- **Personal testimonials:** You have likely worked with people outside of your credit repair company who would be willing to vouch for you. Ask them for a brief testimonial on your work ethic, trustworthiness, or drive to succeed. Prospects will see that you are a reliable person, even if you don't have any testimonials specific to your credit repair company.

- **Testimonials of your expertise:** A great way to get testimonials is by sharing your expertise. If you are knowledgeable about credit repair but do not yet have a client base for testimonials, offer to speak at events or webinars, or offer some free counseling. Afterward, ask individuals in your audience for a testimonial on your expertise. "John is a great resource who is always willing to share his credit repair expertise" is a great testimonial without even needing to make a sale.

- **Share your passion:** Most people get into the credit repair business for personal reasons; either they have repaired their own or family member's credit or have become frustrated with the credit industry. Tell your personal story so people see your passion for credit repair. This personal insight will let people know that you can be trusted.

How To Collect Testimonials

There are three mediums by which to share testimonials:

- **Video:** This is the best way to share a testimonial. People will be able to see the authenticity of the testimonial when your satisfied client is speaking directly to them. Video testimonials do not have to be well produced. In fact, it is often better if they are not. High quality, produced testimonials can seem contrived and inauthentic. Ask a satisfied client if you can shoot a brief video with your cell phone camera, or if they can send you one from their laptop. These are easy and very effective marketing tools.

- **Audio:** Audio testimonials are also effective. Ask a client to call and leave you a voicemail with their testimonial. If you are in-person, record a brief audio bite on your cell phone. Audio testimonials should always be paired up with a genuine photo of the person so that potential clients can see that the testimonial is authentic. As with video, these only need to be 15-30 seconds long, but can be very effective.

- **Text:** If you are unable to get either an audio or video testimonial, a text testimonial is another good option. Like with audio testimonials, they should be paired up with a genuine photo of the client for authenticity.

"When is the best time to capture a testimonial?"

The best time is always right after you have impressed or inspired someone. The longer you wait, the less excited and passionate the testimonial will seem. For example, if you just had five items deleted from a customer's credit report and he emails you to say how impressed he is — that's the time. Reply right away to ask him if he is able to record a short video on his laptop or cell phone talking about what you did, how he feels about it, and how it is helping him reach his goals. You can also incentivize this. Offer that client a free month of services or 20% off for his video testimonial and he will be more than happy to help.

Whether you like it or not, people will research your business before becoming a client, partner, or affiliate. In some cases a lack of information can seem just as untrustworthy as bad reviews. Even if your credit repair company is new, spend some time gathering genuine testimonials so you can control how your company is perceived.

Your Web Site

Do I Need A Website?

Not at all. You can certainly wait by the phone, or walk down the street wearing a sandwich sign…

But if you do want to have a credit repair business website — it does help potential clients see that you're a legitimate credit repair business. Just don't go out there hiring a website developer to build an expensive custom site — it's way too expensive and not necessary. Try an out-of-the box solution that builds an instant credit repair website for you.

The easiest way is to sign up at MyCreditRepairSite.com, because it's quick and easy setup (and we all like quick and easy).

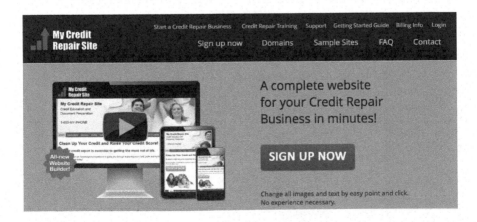

12 Tips For A Killer Website

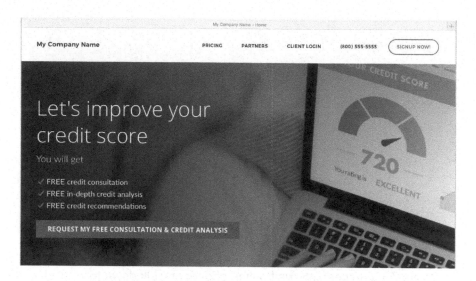

Creating an attractive and effective home page to your site is an art that many new credit repair business owners have a difficult time mastering. When starting a credit repair business, your website can be a great source for lead generation and conversions. However, a home page that is busy, confusing, or vague can be a frustrating waste of money. Below are some tried and true tips from our experts that will help you engage potential customers and grow your business.

First, let's go over the basics.

Your website is a marketing tool that is designed to achieve a single objective: get you qualified leads (people interested in credit repair). Potential customers arrive through a variety of ways — an Internet search result, clicking through one of your advertisements, etc. Once they arrive on the home page, there should be a small amount of information about your business and a big, clear call to action. You should not have information overload and an overwhelming amount of text. The goal is to have a clean, professional, concise, and well-branded page that encourages people to take action.

Remember that your primary goals are to lend legitimacy to your business and to collect leads by entering their contact information into a web form or reaching out to you. Many people also accomplish this by offering a white paper, free trial, coupon, newsletter, or another benefit. Once you have their information, they are added to your sales funnel for your sales team follow up.

If you're a Credit Repair Cloud user, the web lead form will be awesome for this as potential clients fill out the form for your sales team to be *instantly* notified. Remember, this is a "people business" and people will have questions.

So, how do you create a killer home page that generates leads?

1. **Keep it clean:** The page should be attractive, crisp, and clean. There should not be a lot of unnecessary clutter, text, or friction. Get down to the point. Be concise. What should people do and why?

2. **Be consistent with fonts and font sizes, and run a spell check.** Using all different fonts makes a site look cluttered and unprofessional, as do misspelled words. Here's a handy tool for spell checking a website: http://www.internetmarketingninjas.com/online-spell-checker.php.

3. **Drive visitors to request more information or to sign up and pay with a web lead form.** This way, folks who want to know more about your services can request a free consultation with you.

4. **Track impressions:** The goal of your landing page is to generate leads, but how do you know if it's a dud? By installing Google Analytics Tracking Code (A snippet of HTML code that tracks clicks), you will be able to tell how successfully the landing page is converting leads. If it is not performing as well as you'd like, make adjustments. There is no exact formula for a successful landing page: you may have to play around with different features to see what works.

5. **Remember your focal point:** The whole point of the landing page is to persuade a potential client to take action, whether by providing

their contact information, making a purchase, or signing up for a service. Don't let this call to action get lost in an overload of text, photos, or graphics. You can mention this call to action several times, but don't offer several different calls to action or folks will become confused by too many choices. Make it clear and simple so visitors know exactly what they are supposed to do.

6. **Be original with your text.** If you have original text on your site, blog articles, etc., that are relevant and useful, Google will reward you with higher ranking and better placement in search results. Not listed in Google yet? Visit here http://www.google.com/addurl/.

7. **Convey a sense of urgency:** More times than not, if someone leaves your page to "think about it" before taking action, they won't come back. Use words like "Now!" "Right now!" and "Don't miss out!" to make them feel the need to take action before they lose their opportunity.

8. **Display your credibility:** Consumers are getting smarter and more distrustful of marketing ploys. Show that you're not trying to take advantage of them by displaying links to your privacy policy, ethics statement, statistics, quotes, social proof, and other examples of your integrity right on the landing page. Remember that people have different definitions of what makes a company credible, so provide several different examples.

9. **Use directional cues:** Show people where to look. The use of arrows, eyes, pointers, and other directional cues is very effective. If you feature people in your landing page, have their eyes looking toward your call to action. These sorts of subliminal cues will draw attention to where you want it.

10. **Don't forget your phone number:** Some people want to speak to a real person. Listing your phone number clearly make it easy for customers to reach you.

11. **Remember consistency and branding:** Your landing page should have consistent branding to your website and the rest of your

company's public materials. Remember to include your logo, colors, and themes. Your business has a personality which should be consistent across all mediums.

The goal of your marketing efforts is always, ultimately, lead generation. By creating an effective, clean, goal-oriented landing page using the tips above, you can increase leads and grow your business.

If you already have a website, use the tools from your Credit Repair Cloud (see My Company>Web Site Tools). They will work in any website or blog. If you do not have a website, get one today at www.mycreditrepairsite.com.

The Most Important Page On Your Site

So you have a website and are confident that you have every necessary page on it: a contact us page, an affiliate signup page, and maybe even an FAQ page. Those are some _great_ things to have on your website… but there is one page missing, one that will not only help your clients, but will also help you rank better on search engines.*

The page that I am speaking of is your "articles" page. At Credit Repair Cloud, we call this our blog and our knowledge base. Without these pages, we would most likely receive 10x the amount of emails and phone calls than what we currently receive. It wouldn't be too inconvenient to us to get all those emails. However, it would be more inconvenient to our clients to have to reach out to us. By providing the answer to their question in our Knowledge Base, our clients doesn't have to go out of their way to reach out to us and then wait anywhere from 10 minutes to 2 hours to receive a reply.

An article (or "blog") page is a great way to show that you care about your clients, which proves that you have great customer service. This page can have all sorts of articles ranging from "Why is a good score important?" to "Help! I got a letter from the IRS!"

It is important that you not only write articles that your clients will benefit from, but also articles that anyone will benefit from. Providing value is one of the most important job tasks that so many businesses don't care about. If someone researches something on Google and they end up reading your article, there is a high chance that they will browse your website and other articles, they will see that you provide value, and may even become your next client!

So here is a simple equation: Articles (Providing Value) + Trust (and appreciation) = New clients and happy current customers.

It is not a guarantee that you will get on the first page of search engines, but search engines like to see an active website.

Credit Repair Cloud users: Want some awesome videos to display on your site? Just log in to your CRC and click on MY COMPANY>WEB SITE TOOLS.

Scale Faster With Affiliates

The Secret To Getting A Lot Of Affiliate Referrals

Referrals from affiliate partners are one of the best ways to generate leads for your credit repair business—far better, in fact, than taking out expensive ads. However, sometimes, affiliates are difficult to engage. The most common advice you will hear from successful credit repair companies is to make it as easy as possible for your affiliates to send referrals and to show them the benefit of doing so.

Types Of Affiliate Partners

Think of your credit repair business initially as a B2B opportunity. Engaging with affiliate partners is the fastest way to scale your business. There are several types of companies that can be affiliate partners. Think of any type of business that offers financing, such as mortgage brokers, loan officers, and auto dealers, CPAs, tax preparers, debt settlement agencies, bankruptcy attorneys, realtors, etc. These are businesses that have the ability to send you new clients every day.

What To Pay An Affiliate

What you pay affiliates ultimately depends upon your average revenue, but here's an example: If your average client pays you $800-$1200 (or more) over their complete lifecycle with you, it may be advantageous for you to pay an affiliate $50-$120 (or more) for each paid client that they refer to you. That's a 10X return on your investment which is a nice margin. These amounts are up to you, but these are common ranges.

The most successful credit repair companies know that the more generous you are to your affiliates, the more paid clients they will send you. Just one great affiliate can bring you tens of thousands of dollars each year. And, if you keep those clients happy and give them awesome service, they will each tell their friends. That's how your business will start to rapidly scale.

Approaching Potential Affiliates

When approaching any of these businesses, it is crucial to begin with the benefit you can provide them: "a generous commission for each paid client referred, and more qualified buyers that they can close (if they are mortgage brokers, realtors, or auto dealers)."

The first objection you will hear, especially from auto salespeople, is that they don't have time to work with you. They are paid on commission and need to work with as many customers as possible to close sales. However, the reality is that most of the customers who walk in their door will be denied due to credit issues. Show them that while they just spent an hour with a customer who was ultimately denied for financing, they can still earn a generous referral fee by spending two more minutes sending the client to you, or one minute on handing your card, flyer or brochure to that customer. What would normally be a wasted opportunity and wasted time has now become profitable for them.

Providing Talking Points To Your Affiliates

The first thing to provide to affiliates is a concise offer. Think of this as a 60-second elevator pitch. Typically, if a potential customer is turned down for a mortgage or car loan, the loan officer will not offer any alternatives, and they will lose the opportunity to convert this person into a paying customer. Instead, demonstrate value to your affiliates by creating talking points that provide them an opportunity for future business with that customer. Instead of turning a customer away, they can say, "I can approve you for this loan as soon as we are able to improve your credit score." They will then be able to refer the client to your credit repair business.

Make sure that talking points two crucial pieces of information:

1. **Timeframe:** "Most clients are able to achieve a credit score that will allow them to gain approval in X period of time." This is often the first thing that clients will want to know.

2. **Value proposition (where possible):** "I value your business and want to make you a lifetime client. Once we are able to approve your loan, I can credit (half/all of) the cost of this service back to you." You will have to work with the sales manager or sales representative of the affiliate business to see if there is a value proposition they are able to offer the client.

Building Affiliate Relationships

But how do you start to build these affiliate relationships? In most cases, you will have most success meeting with the sales manager or location owner. This person will ultimately make the decision on whether his/her salespeople will work with you and will create a culture that encourages referrals. It helps to have some sort of personal introduction to the business, so tap your network for people who can refer you to local businesses. It is also beneficial to have some level of experience in their industry, whether auto sales, mortgage brokerage, or another kind of financing, so you can speak their language. If you do not have experience, spend time researching the industry before your initial contact.

Additionally, some clever and resourceful credit repair companies have had a great deal of success with having a representative embedded in the physical affiliate business (car dealership, mortgage company, etc.) during high-traffic hours. This way, salespeople can walk the turndowns right over to your representative to get started.

Most importantly, make the referral process as easy as possible for your affiliate salespeople. Automate everything you can through your credit repair software. Data entry is where salespeople often have the most trouble, so make the process seamless and put the majority of the burden on your software. Credit Repair Cloud can make it easy for your affiliates to pass leads onto you through their own affiliate portal, which you can enable for them. Then those leads will appear in your Credit Repair Cloud.

When you do have your meeting, always dress for success from head to toe and carry yourself with confidence. Remember: there's no second chance to make a great first impression.

Closing The Deal With Referrals

Once you've received a referral from an affiliate, it is crucial to act on it as quickly as possible. If a customer is turned down for a loan from one officer, they may go immediately to the next and you will lose the opportunity to engage with them. Your initial conversation is very important because you may only have one chance to close the deal:

1. **Be sincere and engaging.** Find out the customer's pain points: What happened? What is your goal? What is your timeframe, etc?

2. **Be aware of red flags.** No job, no income, no down payment, very low credit score, no computer, etc. You need to be able to understand when you simply can't help a customer and need to refer him/her to someone else in your network (bankruptcy attorneys, etc.) If you are unable to help them, make sure to ask if there is anyone in their family or network who may be able to use your services. There is always an opportunity for new business.

3. **Once you determine the customer is a fit:** update his/her status in to your credit repair software immediately and get the process started.

Building mutually beneficial relationships with affiliate partners, while taking advantage of the wealth of features your credit repair software has to offer, will take your credit repair business to the next level. Credit Repair Cloud has many built-in tools to help strengthen your relationships with your affiliates, including resources for them, easy-to-use forms to pass leads onto you, tools to compensate them, a secure messaging system, etc. Affiliates can add their logo so their clients will see it when they log in and remember who sent them to you.

The most important element that will seal the deal for a long and lucrative relationship is maintaining professionalism and transparency in everything you do. We've built our software with this as our number one goal, and the most successful credit repair companies use these values to their advantage.

Top 5 Ways To Make Your Affiliates Love You

With affiliates potentially bringing you the bulk of your business, it's important to have them love you. To start, let's review where your affiliates come from. They are usually auto dealers, realtors, mortgage brokers, loan officers, CPA's, independent tax preparers, attorneys, insurance agents, and other companies that provide financing to customers.

In most of these industries, there is an approval and denial process, which provides an opportunity for people who are rejected to take advantage of credit repair services. Good for you, but you won't get your affiliates to care unless you show them how referring a client to you can help grow *their* bottom line. By following the steps outlined below you can create lasting, mutually beneficial relationships with your partners and watch both of your businesses grow.

1. **Understand their industry:** Many affiliate partners only get commission on approved applications. It is easy to see why they would not want to take the time to refer people that will not add to their compensation. Therefore, it is important to help these partners see the long-term benefits of your relationship. Make sure to connect customers back to your partners once they are able to get approval. When your partner sees that the business comes back around, they

will be rushing to send more referrals your way!

2. **Think of affiliates as customers:** Many credit repair companies focus on the benefit they provide to end users and not enough on the benefit to affiliate partners. Think of yourself not only as a credit repair company, but also as a marketing and sales resource for your affiliates. When you build a high level of trust with a client, you are also helping build trust between that customer and your affiliate partner.

3. **Co-brand:** Co-brand with your affiliates on communications with customers and create a high level of engagement with both customers and partners. For example, on Credit Repair Cloud's client portal home page you have the opportunity to list your affiliate partner alongside yourself as a primary contact. This will demonstrate to your customers that you and your partner represent a united front. When they are able to reach approval status they will automatically think to return to your affiliate for the next step.

4. **Act as a trusted advisor:** Affiliates do not want to have to turn clients down. Clients are ready and willing to make purchases, but need help in order to do so. Think of yourself as an advisor to your affiliates, helping customers get to a place where they can close the deal. Giving awesome customer service as an advisor will build trust and word of mouth, with each client becoming an ambassador for your business and your affiliate's business.

5. **Use the affiliate tools and portal in your Credit Repair Cloud:** Credit Repair Cloud can help you provide additional value to your affiliate partners through the Client Portal. Some examples of how to best utilize the portal are to direct affiliates to the "Credit Info" and "Resources" pages for educational materials. The more educated your affiliate partners are about credit repair, the better able they will be to support rejected clients as they convert to active clients.

   Your educational resources can help expand your affiliates' spheres of influence and grow their business. List your affiliate partner in your "Resources" page. Your affiliate partner is a valuable resource for the clients that gain approval status and should be treated as such.

Once your affiliate partners see that you are able to add value to their day-to-day operations and their bottom line, you will be able to build strong relationships with each other and with clients — and that's when your revenue will begin to snowball.

Managing Your Team

10 Tips For Motivating Your Employees

Got a team? Many small business owners spend the majority of their time thinking about the external growth of their business and often don't consider whether their employees are motivated and happy. When starting a credit repair business, it can be easy to get wrapped up in finding new clients, building relationships with affiliate partners, learning about new federal regulations, marketing, and the countless other things your business needs to grow. It's easy to lose sight of your office's workplace culture. How can you structure your company in a way that engages employees and makes them feel like part of a functional, cohesive team?

Consider your employees. Do they support each other? Do they collaborate efficiently? Do they seem frequently stressed or nervous? Are they motivated to do well? There are several common "de-motivators" that you may not realize are bringing down your company culture:

1. **Lack of clear goals:** Especially in high-volume environments like the credit repair industry, employees need clear, defined personal and team goals in order to remain motivated. It can be difficult for anyone when the day-to-day work starts to feel mechanical. Goals help provide a north star to keep employees moving in the right direction.

2. **Smothering bosses:** It is easy to understand that small business owners would want to be involved in every decision made in their

company. However, micromanagement is one of the top de-motivators for employees. If your employees feel that you don't trust them to make simple decisions, they will quickly start feeling unimportant and disrespected. Hand over the reigns a little and trust your people. It will make your life easier and your employees happier.

3. **Lopsided teams:** Workplaces need a variety of personality types with a variety of professional strengths. Many small businesses make the mistake of only hiring type-A salespeople because they want to rapidly gain new clients. While these people are great for getting new business, they are often short-term thinkers. Businesses need long-term strategists, operations professionals, and other personalities. Put together a cohesive team so every employee feels important and your business will thrive.

4. **An inadequate or irrelevant compensation system:** Your reward or bonus system should be directly aligned to personal or team goals and should be paid soon after goals are met. Oftentimes, if people are not being rewarded effectively, they will feel unappreciated and unimportant. It is important to make rewards significant, timely, and clear. This will motivate employees to reach their goals; and when they do, they will feel happy and respected.

5. **A bleak work environment:** Do not underestimate the effect your physical office setting has on your employee's' emotional health. If your office is in a bad neighborhood, unclean, dark, or otherwise unattractive, employees' daily mood will be affected. They will not feel proud to work there, and potential clients will be able to tell.

6. **Lack of clear employee and career development:** The types of smart, motivated employees you want to hire will be concerned about their ongoing development. They will feel that if they aren't learning, they aren't growing. Invest in development options for your employees and they will feel like you are interested in their career growth. Make sure to provide a clear career path. Show people the next steps at your company and how they can get there.

7. **Negative people:** Everyone has had these coworkers. Something is always wrong, and no amount of attention will solve it. These employees are toxic to the overall work environment. Try to find out what the underlying issue is and solve it. If that isn't enough, you may have to remove this person for the sake of the rest of the workplace.

8. **Meeting overload:** Meetings can be a great way for employees to discuss and collaborate, but so many companies schedule lots of unnecessary meetings that take employees away from their work and make them feel unfocused. Collaboration for the sake of collaboration can be a huge de-motivator. Make sure all meetings have three crucial components:

    a. Clear, necessary objectives
    b. Actionable follow-up items
    c. Clear start and end times

9. **Fear of failure:** All entrepreneurs know that failure is not always a bad thing; sometimes it takes a few failures to get to a success. The real failure is not trying at all. The same can be said for organic innovation within a workplace. Employees should feel welcome to present new ideas without the fear of being embarrassed if those ideas don't work out. People will feel like they have "skin in the game" if their ideas are heard and your business will thrive from the wealth of fresh ideas.

10. **Lack of strong, transparent leadership:** As the boss all of your employees will look to you as an example of how to behave in the office. It is important to be transparent and reachable. Encourage employees to come to you with ideas or problems. Embody the type of behavior you want from your employees. Give them a kind, motivational role model and they will mirror your actions.

Building a supportive, engaging workplace can be more difficult than it seems. It takes a lot of communication, observation, and transparency to understand what your employees need and figure out how you can give it to them. By following the steps above, you can create a workplace that motivates employees and gives them the tools to do well.

Troubleshooting

Dealing With Stall Tactics From The Bureaus

Many people who are in the beginning stages of starting a credit repair business are daunted by ominously worded stall tactics from credit bureaus. Credit bureaus have begun sending these letters in an attempt to intimidate credit repair companies or individuals into dropping their dispute requests.

It is crucial as the owner of a credit repair company to stand up for the rights of your clients. Stall tactics can typically be divided into two groups: "Suspicious Request" and "Frivolous Request."

Letters From Experian About "A Suspicious Request"

Letters from Experian about a "Suspicious Request"

Have you or your clients received a response letter from Experian like this?

"We received a suspicious request in the mail regarding your personal credit report and determined that it was not sent by you. We will not be initiating any disputes based on the suspicious correspondence."

Here's an explanation:

They don't believe the letter is coming from the client. You may have neglected to include the client's Photo ID and Proof of Address.

Here's a solution:

- Don't send suspicious letters
- Don't use legalese — send the letter as though it's from the client
- Include the client's Photo ID and proof of address
- Never dispute more than 5 items to any bureau within a 30 day period
- If you're a Credit Repair Cloud user, remember to remove our https://www.creditrepaircloud.com web URL from the letter. *See the print page in your software for instructions on correcting that in your web browser settings.*

The simplest fix is to resend the same letter with a handwritten note saying:

> "Oops I'm so sorry, I forgot to include my photo ID and proof of address so you know it's me! Here they are!"
> Draw a little happy face — and be sure to include a new signature plus the ID docs this time!

If it happens again:

You can ask Experian (in a letter from the client) for clarification on what they are considering to be Suspicious, Fraudulent, or Deceptive. That's a fair question to ask and then you'll know what the issue is.

Letters From The Bureaus About "A Frivolous Request"

This stall tactic is based on section 611 of the Fair Credit Reporting Act (FCRA) which states: "A consumer reporting agency may terminate a reinvestigation of information disputed by a customer if the agency reasonably determines that the dispute by the customer is frivolous or irrelevant, including by reason of a failure by a consumer to provide sufficient information to investigate the disputed information."

You'll receive this letter if you've disputed too many items at one time, and we do have letters in the Credit Repair Cloud library that will help you to combat these bureau stall tactics, but it's far better pace yourself to avoid this situation altogether.

If you're just getting started, we recommend not disputing more than five items per bureau, per month. Yes, there are some exceptions where a long laundry list of disputes might be appropriate, for example; a ton of inquiries and new accounts all due to identity theft, but generally speaking, if you send a huge laundry list of disputes all at one time, you risk your disputes being labeled as "frivolous." Once that happens, the bureaus can refuse to investigate your disputes, and you'll waste more time fighting the "frivolous" accusation instead. It's far better to slow down, especially if you're just learning this process. Keep in mind that the most successful credit repair companies only dispute two to three items per month.

There is a secondary benefit to disputing slowly and carefully; sending fewer disputes at a steady pace will also increase your client's life cycle — and, therefore, lifetime value (don't deliberately slow down the process against your client's benefit — just keep it to a pace that gives them the best success rate).

It is important that you not let these types of intimidation techniques bait you into violating the Credit Repair Organizations Act (CROA) by prohibiting your client from contacting the bureau. Just as your client has every right to dispute items on their credit report, they also have every right to contact the bureaus on their own behalf. You can, however, lessen the chance that your client will do something that will undercut their rights by educating them at the beginning of your engagement that these stall tactics may arise and what your response to them will be. Preempt a potential issue by implementing the steps below into your communications pipeline:

- Educate your clients on what a typical stall response looks like and that they are predictable

- Include samples of stall responses in your informational emails and on the Resources page of your credit repair software

- Have your stall response strategy in place and educate consumers about it so there are no surprises

Remember that federal laws exist to protect your clients from being taken advantage of. You are the expert; the more you know about the laws, the more confident and prepared you will be to represent your clients. Your client has rights. By denying your client of these rights, the credit reporting agency can put itself in violation of the Fair Credit Reporting Act (FCRA). Maintain a consistent approach by responding to the stall tactics with the following facts:

- Reassert that all customer ID documents were in place in the original dispute request

- Reiterate the reasons for the dispute and explain that they were clear, conspicuous, and obvious in the original request. Reaffirm the rights of your client

- Notify the bureau that any additional stall tactics will be considered a violation of FCRA

It is important to remember that you are your client's trusted advisor and, in most cases, their only line of defense from being taken advantage of by the credit bureaus. Stand your ground and educate yourself and your clients so that you are prepared to respond to these stall tactics for the most successful outcome possible.

Sample Dispute Letters

If you're a Credit Repair Cloud user, you'll find over 100 dispute letters in your library to cover you for nearly every situation that may arise. You can edit the letters any way you like, and you can add your own. Then when you run the Dispute Wizard, your clients information and the credit item will merge into the letter.

For each item you dispute, you must choose a simple explanation; (the "reason") of why you're disputing an item. You will also need to choose a simple explanation of what you're wanting the bureau to do (the "instructions").

Credit Repair Cloud makes this process ridiculously easy and fast, but if you're not a Credit Repair Cloud user — and you're doing this all manually — here are a few favorite letters to add to your bag of tricks.

Reasons And Instructions

In any dispute letter, it's important to keep things short and simple. Most disputes can be summed up into one sentence. The same rule applies to the instructions for the bureau.

Here are some sample dispute reasons:

- The following personal information is incorrect
- The following account is not mine
- The status is incorrect for the following account
- The following information is outdated. I would like it removed from my credit history report.
- The following inquiry is more than two years old and I would like it removed
- The inquiry was not authorized
- The following accounts were closed by me and should state that
- The following account was a Bankruptcy/Charge-off. Balance should be $0
- Mistaken Identity
- Identity Theft
- This is a duplicate account

- The wrong amount is being reported
- This is the wrong creditor for this item
- Validate Account

Here are some sample instructions:

- Please correct/update this inaccurate information on my credit report.
- Please remove this inaccurate information from my credit report.
- Please remove it from my credit report.
- This is not mine. I am a victim of ID Theft and I have included a police report. Please investigate and remove from my credit report.
- Please supply information on how you have verified this item.
- This is not mine.
- My parent has the same name as me.
- Please investigate and delete from my credit report.
- Please ensure that all information is accurate.

As you can see, they are all simple and to the point. You can add more of your own. No legalese is needed. Just make sure it's the right one for your situation and insert into the appropriate place in the letter.

Credit Bureau Letters

Frequently Used Dispute Letters

If you're a Credit Repair Cloud user, you'll find all the letter samples in this book already included in the 100+ letter library.

The Basic Round 1 Letter

Client's full name
Address
City, State Zip
Phone
Date of Birth
Last 4 of Social Security number:

Previous address (if at current address for less than two years)

Bureau name
Address
City, State Zip

Date

Re: Letter to Remove Inaccurate Credit Information:

To Whom It May Concern:

I received a copy of my credit report and found the following item(s) to be errors:

Creditor
Account number (Example XXXXX1234)
(Reason for the dispute)
(Instructions of what you'd like the bureau to do)
(You can include up to 5 items like this)

By the provisions of the Fair Credit Reporting Act, I demand that these items be investigated and removed from my report. It is my understanding that you will recheck these items with the creditor who has posted them. Please remove any information that the creditor cannot verify. I understand that under 15 U.S.C. Sec. 1681i(a), you must complete this reinvestigation within 30 days of receipt of this letter.

Please send an updated copy of my credit report to the above address. According to the act, there shall be no charge for this updated report. I also request that you please send notices of corrections to anyone who received my credit report in the past six months.

Thank you for your time and help in this matter.

Sincerely,

_____

Client's Name

Credit Repair Cloud users: This is the default Round 1 letter that you would create in Wizard 3. It will work fine as is, but you can certainly personalize it in the letter editor if you'd like to make it more unique. But truth be told, personalizing it is not important. What matters are the facts that you present.

Always remember:

A Round 1 letter is to the bureau(s). It can be about several items, but never more than five (never dispute more than 5 items in a 30 day period).

A Round 2 (or higher) letter is always about just 1 item and it can be written to either a bureau or a creditor. Generally, we start with the bureaus.

Within 30-35 days of sending your initial dispute letter, you will hear back from the credit bureau with the result of your request. The response will be either that your dispute has been confirmed and the item has been deleted or revised, or that the item was confirmed and will remain on your credit report as is.

If your first letter (Round 1) was successful:

If your dispute was confirmed and the bureau made the change you requested, congratulations! Now start another Round 1 letter with the next batch of items (5 items or less) that you wish to dispute.

If your first letter (Round 1) was not successful:

If you could not get the credit bureau to budge, create a letter like the next letter to continue to affirm your dispute and request proof of verification. This is the start of Round 2.

If your first letter (Round 1) got no response at all:

Skip ahead to the non-response letters.

*Credit Repair Cloud users: When you get to Round 2: Use our new "Letter Finder" feature. It will help you choose the perfect letter every time.

Basic Round 2 - The "Prove-It" Letter

This is a Round 2 letter (for a bureau). A Round 2 (or higher) letter is always about just one item. This particular letter is a reply to a bureau that has stated that the item you disputed was "verified." Very often, a bureau will report to you that the item is verified without actually showing you proof. This letter demands that proof. It's called "Dispute After Investigation: The "Prove it" Letter." If you're a Credit Repair Cloud user, you will find this in Wizard 3 Round 2, under "Bureau Letters."

Client's full name
Address
City, State Zip
Phone

Attn: Customer Relations Department
Bureau name
Address
City, State Zip

Date

To Whom It May Concern,

I am in disagreement with the items listed below that still appear on my credit report, even after your Investigation. I would like these items immediately re-investigated. These inaccuracies are highly injurious to my credit rating.

Creditor
Account number (Example XXXXX1234)
(Reason for the dispute)
(Instructions of what you'd like the bureau to do)

Furthermore, In accordance with The Fair Credit Reporting Act, Public law 91-506, Title VI, Section 611, Subsection A-D, please provide the names and business addresses of each individual with whom you verified the above, so that I may follow up.

Please forward me an updated credit report after you have completed your Investigation and corrections.

Your cooperation and prompt attention are greatly appreciated.

Sincerely,

_____

Client's Name

Validate Debt

Within another 30-35 days you should receive another response from the credit bureau with the same potential result: that your dispute was confirmed and deleted, or that the item was confirmed and remains. If the item has not been removed from your report, follow up with a letter like the one below.

Note: As always, each situation is different. If you're a Credit Repair Cloud user, you'll have over 100 letters to choose from.

Client's full name
Address
City, State Zip
Phone

Attn: Customer Relations Department
Bureau name
Address
City, State Zip

(Date)

To Whom It May Concern,
This letter is a formal complaint that you are reporting inaccurate and incomplete credit information.

I am distressed that you have included the information below in my credit profile and that you have failed to maintain reasonable procedures in your operations to assure maximum possible accuracy in the credit reports you publish. Credit reporting laws ensure that bureaus report only 100% accurate credit information. Every step must be taken to assure the information reported is completely accurate and correct. The following information therefore needs to be re-investigated.

Creditor
Account number (Example XXXXX1234)
(Reason for the dispute)

(Instructions of what you'd like the bureau to do)

I respectfully request to be provided proof of this alleged item, specifically the contract, note or other instrument bearing my signature. Failing that, the item must be deleted from the report as soon as possible. The listed item is entirely inaccurate and incomplete, and as such represents a very serious error in your reporting. Please delete this misleading information and supply a corrected credit profile to all creditors who have received a copy within the last six months, or the last two years for employment purposes.

Additionally, please provide the name, address, and telephone number of each credit grantor or other subscriber.

Under federal law, you have thirty (30) days to complete your re-investigation. Be advised that the description of the procedure used to determine the accuracy and completeness of the information is hereby requested as well, to be provided within fifteen (15) days of the completion of your re-investigation.
Sincerely,

_____

Client's Name

Demand To Comply With An Investigation Request

If after another 40 days there is still no change to your credit report, reaffirm your dispute with a more strongly worded letter like this:

Client's full name
Address
City, State Zip
Phone

Attn: Customer Relations Department
Bureau name
Address
City, State Zip

(Date)

To Whom It May Concern,

On (DATE), I wrote to you requesting an investigation into items that I believed were (**Choose**: Inaccurate, outdated or obsolete). To date, I have not received a reply from you or any acknowledgment that an investigation has begun. In my previous request, I listed my reasons for disputing the information. I have enclosed it again and request that you reply within a reasonable amount of time.

Since this is my (second, third, fourth, etc.) request, I will also be sending a copy of this letter to the Federal Trade Commission notifying them that I have signed receipts for letters sent to you and you have not complied with my request. I regret that I am being forced to take such action.

Please see my reasons for dispute below:

Creditor
Account number (Example XXXXX1234)
(Reason for the dispute)
(Instructions of what you'd like the bureau to do)

I also understand that you are required to notify me of your investigation results within 30 days and provide me with an updated copy of my credit report. My contact information is provided below.

Sincerely,

_____

Client's Name

Letter #5
Within 40 days, you will receive yet another response from the credit bureau. If the bureau still refuses to delete the item from your report, send yet another letter referencing the FCRA in order to further dispute your claim.
[Insert Letter 5]

Letter #6
Once again, the bureau will respond to your request after 40 days. The response will be either that your dispute has been confirmed and the item was deleted or that the item will remain. In this sixth and final letter, repeat your complete dispute, including the supporting documentation from the initial letter, so that the dispute will be reinvestigated.

Round 2 (Alternate), If The Bureau Doesn't Respond

Note: If you're a Credit Repair Cloud user, this is a Round 2 letter called "Dispute Follow-up after no response for 30 days." There's also another letter template for 60 days, 90 days, and a few where you threaten to report them to the FTC. If you're a Credit Repair Cloud user, check out the 100+ letters in the library.

Client's full name
Address
City, State Zip

Attn: Customer Relations Department
Bureau name
Address
City, State Zip

Date

To Whom It May Concern,

This letter is formal notice that you have failed to respond in a timely manner to my dispute letter of [insert date], deposited by registered mail with the U.S. Postal Service on that date. Federal law requires you to respond within thirty (30) days, yet you have failed to respond. Failure to comply with these federal regulations by credit reporting agencies are investigated by the Federal Trade Commission (FTC) (see 15 USC 41, et seq.).

I am maintaining a careful record of my communications with you for the purpose of filing a complaint with the FTC should you continue in your non-compliance. I further remind you that, as in Wenger v. Trans Union Corp., No. 95-6445 (C.D.Cal. Nov. 14, 1995), you may be liable for your willful non-compliance.

Be aware that I am making a final goodwill attempt to have you clear up this matter. You have 15 days to cure.

For your benefit, and as a gesture of my goodwill, I will restate my dispute. The following information needs to be verified and, following failure to verify, deleted from the report as soon as possible:

Creditor
Account number (Example XXXXX1234)
(Reason for the dispute)
(Instructions of what you'd like the bureau to do)

The listed item is entirely inaccurate and incomplete, and represents a very serious error in your reporting. Please delete this misleading information and supply a corrected credit profile to all creditors who have received a copy within the last six months, or the last two years for employment purposes.

Additionally, please provide the name, address, and telephone number of each credit grantor or other subscriber.

Under federal law you had thirty (30) days to complete your re-investigation, yet you have failed to respond. Do not delay any further.

Be advised that the description of the procedure used to determine the accuracy and completeness of the information is hereby requested as well, to be provided within fifteen (15) days of the completion of your re-investigation.

Sincerely,

_____

Client's Name

Dispute Follow-Up After No Response For 60 Days

Client's full name
Address
City, State Zip

Attn: Customer Relations Department
Bureau name
Address
City, State Zip

(Date)

To Whom It May Concern,

This letter is formal notice that you have failed to respond in a timely manner to my dispute letter of [insert date], deposited by registered mail with the U.S. Postal Service on that date. Federal law requires you to respond within thirty (30) days, yet you have failed to respond. Failure to comply with these federal regulations by credit reporting agencies are investigated by the Federal Trade Commission (FTC) (see 15 USC 41, et seq.).

I am maintaining a careful record of my communications with you for the purpose of filing a complaint with the FTC should you continue in your non-compliance. I further remind you that, as in Wenger v. Trans Union Corp., No. 95-6445 (C.D.Cal. Nov. 14, 1995), you may be liable for your willful non-compliance.

Be aware that I am making a final goodwill attempt to have you clear up this matter. You have 15 days to cure.

For your benefit, and as a gesture of my goodwill, I will restate my dispute. The following information needs to be verified and, following failure to verify, deleted from the report as soon as possible:

Creditor
Account number (Example XXXXX1234)

(Reason for the dispute)
(Instructions of what you'd like the bureau to do)

The listed item is entirely inaccurate and incomplete, and represents a very serious error in your reporting. Please delete this misleading information and supply a corrected credit profile to all creditors who have received a copy within the last six months, or the last two years for employment purposes.

Additionally, please provide the name, address, and telephone number of each credit grantor or other subscriber.

Under federal law you had thirty (30) days to complete your re-investigation, yet you have failed to respond. Do not delay any further. Be advised that the description of the procedure used to determine the accuracy and completeness of the information is hereby requested as well, to be provided within fifteen (15) days of the completion of your re-investigation.

Sincerely,

_____
Client's Name

Intention To File FTC Complaint - After 30 Days

Client's full name
Address
City, State Zip

Attn: Customer Relations Department
Bureau name
Address
City, State Zip

(Date)

To Whom It May Concern,

This letter shall serve as formal notice of my intent to file a complaint with the FTC, due to your blatant and objectionable disregard of the law. As indicated by the attached copies of letters and mailing receipts, you have received and accepted through registered mail my dispute letter dated [date], as well as my follow-up letter dated [date]. To date you have not done your duty as mandated by law. Your non-compliance with federal law is unacceptable; your disregard for it contemptible. Rest assured that I shall hold you accountable.

Federal law requires you to respond within 30 days, yet you have failed to respond. Failure to comply with these federal regulations by credit reporting agencies are investigated by the Federal Trade Commission (see 15 USC 41, et seq.).

I am maintaining a careful record of my communications with you on this matter for the purpose of filing a complaint with the FTC should you continue in your non-compliance. I further remind you that, as in Wenger v. Trans Union Corp., No. 95-6445 (C.D.Cal. Nov. 14, 1995), you may be liable for your willful noncompliance.

For the record, the following information is being erroneously included on my credit report, as I have advised you on two separate occasions, more than 75 days and again 40 days ago:

Creditor
Account number (Example XXXXX1234)
(Reason for the dispute)
(Instructions of what you'd like the bureau to do)

If you do not immediately remove this inaccurate and incomplete information, I will file a formal complaint with the Federal Trade Commission.

Should you continue to operate with complete disregard for the law, I intend to seek redress in civil action for recovery of damages, costs, and attorney fees. For this purpose I am carefully documenting these events, including the lack of response REQUIRED under law from you. Additionally, please provide the name, address, and telephone number of each credit grantor or other subscriber.

Under federal law, you had 30 days to complete your re-investigation, yet you have failed to respond. Further delays are inexcusable.

Be advised that the description of the procedure used to determine the accuracy and completeness of the information is hereby requested as well, to be provided within 15 days of the completion of your re-investigation.

Sincerely,

_____

Client's Name

Intent To File Lawsuit For FCRA Violation

Client's full name
Address
City, State Zip

Attn: Customer Relations Department
Bureau name
Address
City, State Zip

(Date)

Re: Intent To File Lawsuit for FCRA Violation

To Whom It May Concern,

It is a crime to threaten lawsuit with no intention of doing so, therefore you can take heed that I am very serious about filing suit against your company. I have sent [NUMBER OF LETTERS] previous letters to you, all by certified mail (receipts enclosed), requesting that you remove inaccurate information from my file, and you have failed to do so.

Accordingly, I can show a judge that these accounts are inaccurate and that you violated the Fair Credit Reporting Act by ignoring my requests to investigate the items. My previous letters (all sent by certified mail) stated my reasons for an investigation and these reasons were not frivolous in any way.

If this final request does not prompt you to conduct a proper investigation of these accounts in question and send proof to me of said investigation, I will file a civil suit in my county for damages and you can travel to defend yourself.

I take my credit very seriously and your lack of professionalism and assistance disappoints me. I am well aware of my rights under the Fair Credit Reporting Act and I intend to pursue them to the maximum.

I await your response.

Sincerely,

_____

Client's Name

cc: Federal Trade Commission; Attorney General

Request Removal After Creditor Verification

Client's full name
Address
City, State Zip

Attn: Customer Relations Department
Bureau name
Address
City, State Zip

(Date)

Re: Creditor Verification of incorrect items on my credit history report.
Credit Report Number:

To Whom It May Concern,

On (DATE), I received my credit report from you. It included the following incorrect information:

Creditor
Account number (Example XXXXX1234)
(Reason for the dispute)
(Instructions of what you'd like the bureau to do)

I am enclosing a copy of my credit report with the incorrect data highlighted. I just received a letter from that creditor verifying that this information on my credit report is inaccurate and should be removed from my credit file. I have enclosed a copy of the letter.

[OR]

On (DATE) I spoke with (CONTACT PERSON) from . This person verified that this information on my credit report is indeed inaccurate and should be removed from my credit file.

Creditor

Account number (Example XXXXX1234)
(Reason for the dispute)
(Instructions of what you'd like the bureau to do)

You can reach this person at (CONTACT NUMBER)

I am enclosing a copy of my credit report with the incorrect data highlighted. This incorrect and negative information is damaging my credit. Please remove this incorrect information at once and send me an updated copy of my credit history report.I also request that you please send notices of corrections to anyone who received my credit report in the past six months.

Thank you for your time and help in this matter.

Sincerely,

_____

Client's Name
cc: Federal Trade Commission

(ENCLOSE A COPY OF CREDIT REPORT WITH THE INCORRECT ITEMS IN QUESTION HIGHLIGHTED. ALSO INCLUDE ALL OTHER DOCUMENTATION VERIFYING THE ABOVE FACTS)

"Frivolous Dispute" Response

Occasionally, your client may receive a response that calls your disputes "frivolous." We see this happen most often if you're disputing too many items. Remember to keep them under 5 dispute items per month. When that frivolous letter comes, here's a great response.

Client's full name
Address
City, State Zip

Attn: Customer Relations Department
Bureau name
Address
City, State Zip

(Date)

To Whom It May Concern,

I received a letter from your firm stating that my letter requesting verification of erroneous items on my report as being classified as "frivolous" or "irrelevant." I assure you that in no way do I consider a matter of such importance to me as frivolous nor irrelevant. In fact, if you do not honor my original request to verify the items contained in my previous letter, mailed (DATE SENT) via certified mail, I will file a complaint with the Federal Trade Commission against your company.

I have included my original disputes for your convenience below:
The following information therefore needs to be reinvestigated. I respectfully request to be provided proof of this alleged item, specifically the contract, note, or other instrument bearing my signature. Failing that, the items must be deleted from the report as soon as possible:

Creditor
Account number (Example XXXXX1234)
(Reason for the dispute)
(Instructions of what you'd like the bureau to do)

(add the other items if this was in response to a Round 1 letter about multiple items)

The listed item is completely inaccurate and incomplete, and is a very serious error in reporting. Please delete this misleading information, and supply a corrected credit profile to all creditors who have received a copy within the last 6 months, or the last 2 years for employment purposes. Additionally, please provide the name, address, and telephone number of each credit grantor or other subscriber.

Under federal law, you have 30 days to complete your reinvestigation. Be advised that the description of the procedure used to determine the accuracy and completeness of the information is hereby requested as well. Please provide this information within 15 days of the completion of your reinvestigation.

Sincerely,

_____

Client's Name

Reply To Accusation Of Credit Repair

Sometimes a Credit Bureau will accuse you of using a credit repair company (which is your right by law). Here is a letter to put them in their place and to avoid slowing down your disputes.

Client's full name
Address
City, State Zip

Attn: Customer Relations Department
Bureau name
Address
City, State Zip

(Date)

To Whom It May Concern,

Please be advised that I have received your computer-generated letter stating that you have ceased investigation of my credit reports because, in your opinion, you believe that I have used a third party credit repair agency. Not only do I believe this to be a stall tactic on your part to grant you an additional 30 days to comply with my original request, but I believe it to be a blatant violation of the FCRA.

You were advised by me on [insert date] by certified mail (copy enclosed) that I questioned the accuracy of a few items on my credit reports. That request was written by me and mailed by me — not a third party agency. I also included my photo ID and Proof of Address. It appears obvious to me that you are abusing your power under the FCRA to avoid a complete investigation.

Here again is the incorrect information being reported:

Creditor
Account number (Example XXXXX1234)
(Reason for the dispute)

(Instructions of what you'd like the bureau to do)

Additionally, there is NO law that states a consumer cannot use a third party, so using that as your excuse is irrelevant. In fact, the United States Congress has found the whole process so overwhelming that they afford consumers the right to use a third party on their behalf if the consumer so chooses. This is why your statement is so shameful.

I reserve the right to sue a credit bureau for violations of the Fair Credit Reporting Act and I believe I can prove that you did not use reasonable measures to insure the accuracy of my credit reports and now you are stalling the process even further.

I realize that disputes can be expensive and it is your job to stall them, but you do so at great risk. Please take notice that this letter dated [insert today's date] is a formal notice to you that I am requesting you to continue forward with my original investigation request and please send the results to me within 15 days. I therefore legally and lawfully refuse your "form letter," thus giving you only 15 days not 30 more.

I am annoyed and outraged at your accusation, and I have researched my rights in regard to my credit file. Please expedite my original request immediately.

Sincerely,

_____

Client's Name

Creditor Letters

Goodwill Deletion

Here's a sample request for Goodwill Deletion letter for a creditor.

Client's full name
Address
City, State Zip

Creditor name
Address
City, State Zip

(Date)

Re: (Account number)

To Whom It May Concern,

I was advised to write to you by your customer service department concerning my credit rating with your company. I have been a [company name] customer since [date] and during that time, I have enjoyed my account with you greatly.

I'm writing to ask if you would be willing to make a "goodwill" adjustment to your reporting to the three credit bureaus. I have X late payments on my account that are from back in [date]. Since that time, I have been an exceptional customer, paying every month on time. Because of my exceptional payment history over the last X years, I would like you to consider removing the X late payments from my credit report.

At the time of the X lates, I was in a financial dilemma due to (job loss, health issues, new baby, etc.). I am not writing this to justify why the payments were late, but rather to show that the late payments are not a good indicator of my actual credit worthiness. I hope that [Company name] is willing to work with me on erasing this mark from my credit reports. I have been a very happy customer for all these years and hope to continue a long relationship with [Company name].

The credit bureaus have advised me that they can remove the lates if they are instructed to by you, but they need to have that instruction in writing. Your customer service representative suggested that I write to you for a "Goodwill Adjustment." I beg that you may help me and take into consideration how good of a customer I have been and how long I have had an account with you.

Please let me know if there is any additional documentation that would help in reaching a positive outcome, and I thank you again for the time you have spent in reading this letter.

Sincerely,

_____

Client's Name

Pay For Delete (Offer Payment If Negative Items Are Removed)

Client's full name
Address
City, State Zip

Creditor name
Address
City, State Zip

[Date]

Re: [Account number]

On [Date], I received a copy of my credit report from [Credit Bureau Name]. That report lists my payments to you as being 'delinquent.' My financial problems are now behind me and I am in a position to pay off this debt. I can pay a lump sum amount of $_____ or I can pay installments in the amount of $_____ per month for _____ months if you will agree to one of the following:

( ) If I make a lump sum payment, you will agree to remove all negative information from my credit file associated with the debt.

( ) If I agree to pay off the debt in monthly installments, you agree to 're-age' my account — making the current month the first repayment month and showing no late payments as long as I make the agreed upon monthly payments.

If this offer is acceptable to you, please check and initial one of the above choices, sign your acceptance below and return this letter to me in the enclosed envelope.

Thank you for your time and assistance.

Sincerely,

_____

Client's Name

Agreed to and accepted to on this _____ day of _____.

By: _____

(Creditor Representative Signature)

Name (print): _____

Company:_____

Title:_____

Debt Settlement Offer To Dismiss Court Judgment

Client's full name
Address
City, State Zip

Creditor name
Address
City, State Zip
Re: (Account number)

To: Judgment Creditor, {creditor_name}
From: Judgment Debtor, {client_first_name} {client_last_name}
Case number: (CASE NUMBER)
Judgment amount: (AMOUNT)

(Date)

Dear Sir,

I am aware of the money due you and of the judgment placed against me for this money. I had every intention of taking care of this prior to the entry of the judgment, but unfortunately time constraints ended that chance.

Today I am writing to you so that we may put this matter behind us and settle out this judgment for good, under a few conditions. This will save you time and money trying to collect the judgment and will help me recover from your negative entry against me.

I have been offered an amount from a close family member to pay you $ (AMOUNT) to settle the debt in full and have the judgment dismissed.

As the judgment creditor, you reserve the right to dismiss or vacate the judgment as well as entering it. If I pay you from this offer letter saving you immense time, fees, and paperwork, you can then file a simple paper with the courts dismissing the judgment.

My offer is to pay you in exchange for the dismissal so that we have both gained something from this unfortunate situation. It is extremely important that you dismiss the judgment rather than satisfying it, because a satisfied judgment really looks no better for me than a filed judgment.

With a dismissed judgment, I can justify paying you. Upon your signed approval of this offer, I will forward the full settlement to you immediately. I understand this offer is void if I do not send you $(AMOUNT) within 5-10 days of your signed confirmation.

If you agree to "dismiss" the judgment upon full and final payment of $ (AMOUNT), then please sign and return this offer and acceptance.

Offer Accepted and Agreed,

_____
Judgment Creditor Signature   Date

_____
Judgment Creditor Authorized Representative
On behalf of:

_____
Judgment Creditor Company Name

Debt Settlement Offer

If you have effectively agreed with a creditor or collector to settle a debt, this letter will to secure your rights for amount to be paid and credit reporting issues. Do not use this letter if the debt is disputed or expired, as doing so can renew the statute of limitations. If you agree that the debt is valid and you wish to begin negotiations you may also use this letter to present your first offer.

Re: Debtor's Settlement

Client's full name
Address
City, State Zip

Creditor name
Address
City, State Zip

(Date)

Re: (Account number)

To Whom It May Concern:

I understand that I owe a balance to your company. This letter is an offer to settle the debt for less because of my inability to pay the entire balance. Because of dire financial circumstances, [overwhelming debt, loss of job, insurance settlement with limited funds, considering bankruptcy, borrowing the money, illness, loss of family member with income, etc. List your reason here as to why you are offering to pay less.] I am only able to pay a portion of this debt.

I recognize you may be motivated as well, because of the age of the debt and because of my financial crisis. Declining to work with me will only make matters worse for both of us.

You are claiming the amount owed on the account is $_____. Please accept my good faith offer to settle this account under these following conditions ONLY:

The parties involved agree to settle the account in full for the sum of $_____ and this amount is accepted as complete and final payment on said debt. Full discharge and settlement of all monies due will be created, provided that the amount agreed upon shall be paid as follows:

Payment terms: how debt will be paid, (i.e., three payments of $250.00 to be paid monthly on the 1st of each month, 8 payments of $200.00 on the 1st of each month after execution of this agreement, etc.)
Payment address: where you will send payment each month.
Other terms: list specific arrangements made, such as, creditor agrees to freeze the account without any additional fees or interest added to the balance, etc.

Credit reporting: list all account status terms you are requesting such as "paid in full," "deleted," "settled in full," "settled for less," etc.

Governing states: This agreement shall be binding under the laws of [list your state and the creditor's state].

If your office is in agreement with this settlement, please reply with confirmation on your company letterhead and signed by an individual with the authority to accept such offers. Time is of the essence because of my financial situation, so please reply as soon as possible.

Kind regards,

_____

Client's Name

Cashed Check Constitutes Payment In Full

(This letter is in 2 parts. Delete the sections that you don't need.)

Client's full name
Address
City, State Zip

Creditor name
Address
City, State Zip

(Date)

Re: (Account number)

To Whom It May Concern:

This letter concerns the money I owe you. I have received bills from you stating that I owe (AMOUNT OF BILL). However, I am disputing the amount owed to you because of the following reasons:

(LIST REASONS FOR DISPUTE)

I feel I owe you no more than $(ENTER AMOUNT). It is obvious that there is a good faith dispute over this bill.

To settle this debt, I will send you a check for $(ENTER AMOUNT) with a restrictive endorsement; if you cash that check it will constitute an accord and satisfaction. In other words; you will receive from me a check that states "cashing of this check constitutes payment in full." If you cash this check, that check will clear away any debt that I owe you.

If agreed, please sign and return this letter.
Thank you for your time and assistance.

Sincerely yours,

_____

Client's Name

Agreed to and accepted to on this _____ day of _____,
_____.

By:

_____
(Creditor Representative's Signature)
Name (print):_____
Title (print):_____
Company (print):_____

LETTER 2 (OF 2) TO BE SENT WITH YOUR CHECK** (AFTER 30 DAYS):

Client's full name
Address
City, State Zip

Creditor name
Address
City, State Zip

(Date)

To Whom It May Concern:

Enclosed is a check for $ (Amount) to cover the balance of Account Number: {account_number}.

This check is tendered in accordance with my letter dated (Date of First Letter). If you cash this check, you agree that my debt has been paid off in full.

Sincerely yours,

_____
Client's Name

(**Important: Write on the bottom of the check on the front along the top or bottom the exact language you used in the second letter "This check is tendered in accordance with my letter of (DATE OF FIRST LETTER). If you cash this check you agree that my debt is paid in full.")

Validation Of Debt (After Dispute To Bureau)

Client's full name
Address
City, State Zip

Creditor name
Address
City, State Zip

(Date)

Re: (Account number)

To Whom It May Concern,

Your company is reporting the below referenced account on my credit report as a collection account.

{dispute_item_and_explanation}

I have disputed this item with the credit reporting agency and they reported you confirmed the account as valid.

In a good faith effort to resolve the matter amicably, I must demand proof of this debt, specifically the alleged contract or other instrument bearing my signature, as well as proof of your authority in this matter. Absent such proof, you must correct any erroneous reports of this past debt as mine.

I am writing to request that you please provide the following information:

1. Please evidence your authorization under 15 USC 1692(e) and 15 USC 1692(f) in this alleged matter.
2. What is your authorization of law for your collection of information?
3. What is your authorization of law for your collection of this alleged debt?

4. Please evidence your authorization to do business or operate in this state.
5. Please evidence proof of the alleged debt, including the alleged contract or other instrument bearing my signature.
6. Please provide a complete account history, including any charges added for collection activity.

You have thirty (30) days from receipt of this notice to respond. Failure to respond in writing, hand-signed, and in a timely manner, will be considered a waiver to any and all of your claims in this matter, and will entitle me to presume you placed this on my credit report(s) in error and that this matter is permanently closed. Provide the proof, or correct the record and remove this invalid debt from all sources to which you have reported it.

For the purposes of 15 USC 1692 et seq., this Notice has the same effect as a dispute to the validity of the alleged debt and a dispute to the validity of your claims. This Notice is an attempt to correct your records, and any information received from you will be collected as evidence should further action be necessary. This is a request for information only, and is not a statement, election, or waiver of status.

Client's Full Name

(DO NOT SIGN)

Validation Of Debt

Client's full name
Address
City, State Zip

(Name of Collection Agency)
Address
City, State Zip

(Date)

Re: Account number.

To [person whose name appears on agency's notice to you]:

This letter is a formal complaint that you are reporting inaccurate and incomplete credit information.

I am distressed that you have included the information below in my credit profile and that you have failed to maintain reasonable procedures in your operations to assure maximum possible accuracy in the credit reports you publish. Credit reporting laws ensure that bureaus report only 100% accurate credit information. Every step must be taken to assure the information reported is completely accurate and correct. The following information therefore needs to be re-investigated.

I respectfully request to be provided proof of this alleged item, specifically the contract, note, or other instrument bearing my signature. Failing that, the item must be deleted from the report as soon as possible. The listed item is entirely inaccurate and incomplete, and as such represents a very serious error in your reporting. Please delete this misleading information and supply a corrected credit profile to all creditors who have received a copy within the last six months, or the last two years for employment purposes.

Additionally, please provide the name, address, and telephone number of each credit grantor or other subscriber.

Under federal law, you have thirty (30) days to complete your re-investigation. Be advised that the description of the procedure used to determine the accuracy and completeness of the information is hereby requested as well, to be provided within fifteen (15) days of the completion of your re-investigation.

Sincerely,

_____

Client's name

Validation Of Debt (Estoppel By Silence)

(Doctrine of Estoppel by Silence can be extremely powerful with collection agencies that have ignored your Validation of Debt requests. According to Black Law, the meaning is: Estoppel - A legally imposing bar resulting from one's own conduct and precluding any denial assertion regarding a fact. A doctrine that prevents a person from adopting an inconsistent position, attitude or action if it will result in injury to another. An affirmative defense alleging good faith. Estoppel by Silence: Estoppel that arises when a party is under a duty to speak but fails to. The Estoppel letter is used when you request Validation of Debt and do not get a response from the Collection Agency. It uses the "Doctrine of Estoppel" which tells the collection agency that their silence must mean they agree with you. This letter can be used after you have already sent two Validation of Debt requests to a collection agency.)

Client's full name
Address
City, State Zip

(Name of Collection Agency)
Address
City, State Zip

(Date)

To [person whose name appears on agency's notice to you]:

Re: Account number:

This certified letter, receipt number: _____ is to formally advise you that I believe your company has violated several of my consumer rights. Specifically:

You failed to validate a debt at my request, which is a FDCPA violation and you continued to report a disputed debt to the Credit Bureaus: another FCRA violation

Not only have you ignored my prior requests for validation of debt (proof attached: receipt copies or letter copies) but you continue to report this debt to the credit bureaus, causing damage to my character. This letter will again request that you follow the FDCPA and please provide the following:

Validation of Debt Request

-Proof of your right to own/collect this alleged debt
-Balance claimed including all fees, interest and penalties
-Contract bearing my personal signature

As you may be aware, "Estoppel by Silence" legally means that you had a duty to speak but failed to do so, therefore, that must mean you agree with me that this debt is false. I will use the Estoppel in my defense.

I expect to receive the proof requested above within 15 days of this letter. Should you again ignore my request for validation of debt I reserve the right to sue your company for violations of my consumer rights as specified under both the FDCPA and the FCRA. I may also seek damages from you if warranted.

Kind regards,

_____

Client's name

Warning Violation For Expired Debt Collection

Client's full name
Address
City, State Zip

(Name of Collection Agency)
Address
City, State Zip

(Date)

To [person whose name appears on agency's notice to you]:

Re: Account number:

Please be advised that you are attempting to collect on an expired debt. I am invoking my right to cease you, based on factual law that this debt in question is legally expired under the Statute of Limitations. Accordingly, I am requesting that you do not attempt to collect this expired debt, and should you seek legal recourse I will invoke my right of the expired statute as a valid defense.

Additionally any attempts to harm my credit history and rating by updating or changing dates after you have been informed that the debt is expired, is a direct violation of the FDCPA. Any abuse to my credit rating on your part will be met with all recourse available to me by the law. I am aware of how long items may remain on my credit reports and any attempt to extend the reporting time will be investigated by me, and reported to my State Attorney General and the American Collectors Association.

I am completely aware of how long the debt may be legally collectable and how long it may be legally reportable. I realize a debt is allowed to be reported on my credit history for no longer than 7 years, and my research has shown me that often a collection agency will reset the date of original charge off to the date they purchased it, thus trying to extend

the reporting time in an attempt to force a consumer into paying it. I am informing you of this knowledge so that you may do the right thing.
I have no intentions of renewing the expired statute of limitations, so please stop wasting your time contacting me. I expect this will be the last time I hear from you.

Sincerely,

_____
Client's name

Temporarily Stop Collections

Client's full name
Address
City, State Zip

(Name of Collection Agency)
Address
City, State Zip

(Date)

To [person whose name appears on agency's notice to you]:

Thank you for your recent inquiry. This is not a refusal to pay, but a notice that your claim is being disputed. This is a request for validation made pursuant to the Fair Debt Collection Practices Act.

Be advised that I am not requesting a "verification" that you have my mailing address, I am requesting a "validation;" that is, competent evidence that I have some contractual obligation to pay you.

You should also be aware that sending unsubstantiated demands for payment through the United States Mail System might constitute mail fraud under federal and state law. You may wish to consult with a competent legal advisor before your next communication with me. Your failure to satisfy this request within the requirements of the Fair Debt Collection Practices Act will be construed as your absolute waiver of any and all claims against me, and your tacit agreement to compensate me for costs and attorney fees.

Sincerely,

_____

Client's name

Cease And Desist

Client's full name
Address
City, State Zip

(Name of Collection Agency)
Address
City, State Zip

(Date)

To Whom It May Concern:

Re: Notice to Cease Contact, Case # (ENTER CASE NUMBER IF AVAILABLE, PLUS CREDITOR INFORMATION AND ACCOUNT NUMBER)

To (PERSON WHOSE NAME APPEARS ON THE AGENCY'S NOTICE TO YOU):

(CHOOSE ONE)

Since approximately _____, I have received several phone calls and letters from you concerning an overdue account with the above-named creditor.

(OR)

On (date) I received written notice of the claimed debt, a copy of which is attached.

This is to give you notice to cease all contact with me or anyone else except the creditor about this claimed debt. Accordingly, under 15 U.S.C. Sec. 1692c, this is my formal notice to you to cease all further communications with me. If you must contact me, please do so in writing and not by telephone.

I look forward to your acknowledgement that you have received this notice by [insert a date that is two weeks from the date of this letter].

Sincerely,

_____

Client's

Sample Agreement And Client Intake Docs

This is the default agreement from Credit Repair Cloud. It contains the following parts: Credit Repair Service Agreement, Authorization for Credit Repair Action (this is what most people use instead of a Power of Attorney), plus Consumer Credit File Rights, CROA Disclosure, Right Of Cancellation Notice and State Specific Disclosures (if applicable).

Agreement

{COMPANY NAME}
{COMPANY ADDRESS}
{COMPANY CITY}, {COMPANY STATE} {COMPANY POSTCODE}

Prepared for:

{CLIENT NAME}
{CLIENT ADDRESS}
{CLIENT CITY}, {CLIENT STATE} {CLIENT POSTCODE}
{TODAYS DATE}

The following pages contain:
1. Credit Repair Service Agreement
2. Authorization for Credit Repair Action
3. Consumer Credit File Rights (CROA Disclosure)
4. Right Of Cancellation Notice
5. State Specific Disclosures (add if applicable)

Credit Repair Service Agreement for {CLIENT NAME}

I, {CLIENT NAME}, hereby enter into the following agreement with {COMPANY NAME}.

{COMPANY NAME} hereby agrees to perform the following:

1. To evaluate Customer's current credit reports as listed with applicable credit reporting agencies and to identify inaccurate, erroneous, false, or obsolete information. To advise Customer as

to the necessary steps to be taken on the part of Customer in conjunction with Our Company, to dispute any inaccurate, erroneous, false or obsolete information contained in the customer's credit reports.

2. To prepare all necessary correspondence in dispute of inaccurate, erroneous, false, or obsolete information in customer's credit reports.

3. To review credit profile status from the credit reporting agencies such as: Experian, Equifax and Transunion. Consulting, coaching, and monitoring services are conducted by personal meetings, webinars, video conferenclng, telephone, email, or by any other form of communication during normal business hours.

In exchange, I, {CLIENT NAME}, agree to pay the following fees as outlined in the following fee schedule:

1. $_____ at signup for document processing
2. $_____ at the start of each new month of service.

Authorization For Credit Repair Action

1. I, {CLIENT NAME}, hereafter known as "client" hereby authorize, {COMPANY NAME}, {COMPANY ADDRESS}, {COMPANY CITY}, {COMPANY STATE} {COMPANY ZIP CODE}, to make, receive, sign, endorse, execute, acknowledge, deliver, and possess such applications, correspondence, contracts, or agreements as necessary to improve my credit. Such instruments in writing of whatever and nature shall only be effective for any or all of the three credit reporting agencies which are TransUnion, Experian, Equifax, and any other reporting agencies or creditor's listed, as may be necessary or proper in the exercise of the rights and powers herein granted.

2. This authorization may be revoked by the undersigned at any time by giving written notice to the party authorized herein. Any

activity made prior to revocation in reliance upon this authorization shall not constitute a breach of rights of the client. If not earlier revoked, this authorization will automatically expire twelve months from the date of signature.

3. The party named above to receive the information is not authorized to make any further release or disclosure of the information received. This authorization does not authorize the release or disclosure of any information except as provided herein.

4. I grant to {COMPANY NAME}, {COMPANY ADDRESS}, {COMPANY CITY}, {COMPANY STATE} {COMPANY ZIP CODE}, authority to do, take, and perform, all acts and things whatsoever requisite, proper, or necessary to be done, in the exercise of repairing my credit with the three credit reporting agencies, which are TransUnion, Experian, Equifax, and any other reporting agencies or creditors listed, as fully for all intents and purposes as I might or could do if personally present.

5. I hereby release {COMPANY NAME}, {COMPANY ADDRESS}, {COMPANY CITY}, {COMPANY STATE} {COMPANY ZIP CODE}, from all and all matters of actions, causes of action, suits, proceedings, debts, dues, contracts, judgments, damages, claims, and demands whatsoever in law or equity, for or by reason of any matter, cause, or thing whatsoever as based on the circumstances of this contract.

Consumer Credit File Rights Under State And Federal Law

You have a right to dispute inaccurate information in your credit report by contacting the credit bureau directly. However, neither you nor a credit repair company or credit repair organization has the right to have accurate, current and verifiable information removed from your credit report. The credit bureau must remove accurate, negative information from your report only if it is over 7 years old. Bankruptcy information can be reported up to 10 years.

You have a right to obtain a copy of your credit report from a credit bureau. You may be charged a reasonable fee. There is no fee, however, if you have been turned down for credit, employment, insurance, or a rental dwelling because of information in your credit report within the preceding 60 days. The credit bureau must provide someone to help you interpret the information in your credit file. You are entitled to receive a free copy of your credit report if you are unemployed and intend to apply for employment in the next 60 days, if you are a recipient of public welfare assistance, or if you have reason to believe that there is inaccurate information in your credit report due to fraud.

You have a right to sue a credit repair organization that violated the Credit Repair Organization Act. This law prohibits deceptive practices by credit repair organizations.

You have the right to cancel your contract with any credit repair organization for any reason within 3 business days from the date you signed it.

Credit bureaus are required to follow reasonable procedures to ensure that the information they report is accurate. However, mistakes may occur.

You may, on your own, notify a credit bureau in writing that you dispute that accuracy of information in your credit file. The credit bureau must then reinvestigate and modify or remove inaccurate or incomplete information. The credit bureau may not charge any fee for this service. Any pertinent information and copies of all documents you have concerning an error should be given to the credit bureau.

If the credit bureau's reinvestigation does not resolve the dispute to your satisfaction, you may send a brief statement to the credit bureau to be kept in your file, explaining why you think the record is inaccurate. The credit bureau must include a summary of your statement about disputed information with any report it issues about you.

The Federal Trade Commission regulates credit bureaus and credit repair organizations. For more information, contact: The Public Reference Branch Federal Trade Commission Washington, D.C. 20580.

Notice Of Right To Cancel

You may cancel this contract, without any penalty or obligation, at any time before midnight of the 3rd day which begins after the date the contract is signed by you.

To cancel this contract, mail or deliver a signed, dated copy of this cancellation notice, or any other written notice to {COMPANY NAME}, {COMPANY ADDRESS}, {COMPANY CITY}, {COMPANY STATE} {COMPANY ZIP CODE}, before midnight on the 3rd day which begins after the date you have signed this contract stating "I hereby cancel this transaction, (date) (purchaser's signature).

Please acknowledge your receipt of this notice by electronically signing the form indicated below.

Acknowledgment Of Receipt Of Notice

I, {CLIENT NAME}, hereby acknowledge with my digital signature, receipt of the Notice of Right to Cancel. I confirm the fact that I agree and understand what I am signing, and acknowledge that I have received a copy of my Consumer Credit File Rights.

Client Recommendations

This is completely optional, but It's a nice handout to give a new client. It lets them know how credit repair works and what they can do to speed up the process.

{COMPANY LOGO}
{COMPANY NAME}
{COMPANY ADDRESS}
{COMPANY CITY}, {COMPANY STATE} {COMPANY ZIP CODE}

Prepared for:

{CLIENT NAME}
{CLIENT ADDRESS}
{CLIENT CITY}, {CLIENT STATE} {CLIENT ZIP CODE}
{TODAYS DATE}

Client Information and Recommendations:

As your credit specialist, our most important job is to review your credit history reports with you and to begin process of disputing negative inaccurate items on your reports. Our next important job is to give you recommendations to follow, which will help you speed up the process, achieve a higher score and keep it. While we do our part, please take the following steps and your score will start to improve very quickly.

How does credit repair work? Is it legal?

Credit repair is 100% legal. It works because of a law called "The Fair Credit Reporting Act." The FCRA gives you the right to dispute any item on your credit report. If that item cannot be verified within a reasonable time (usually 30 days) it must be removed. Even accurate negative items can often be removed or negotiated away. This law is the basis of all credit repair and the foundation of our business.

FAQs

Where Can I Get Credit Repair Training?

Get a training and a certificate at CreditHeroChallenge.com.

Is Credit Repair Legal?

Yes, credit repair is legal and it works because of the law. The law is the Fair Credit Reporting Act, which was created by the FTC to protect consumers. The FCRA gives you the right to dispute any item on a credit report. If that item cannot be verified it must be removed. That is the foundation of all credit repair. Credit Repair is also regulated with it's own set of laws called CROA, The "Credit Repair Organizations Act" which spells out how credit repair businesses may operate.

How Does Credit Repair Work?

You identify issue on the reports and send dispute letters to the bureaus. If the items cannot be verified, they must be removed. Additionally, you'll provide education to your clients to do their part to speed up the process and maintain their good credit long after your work is done.

What Does It Cost To Start A Credit Repair Business?

This is a very affordable startup. The most important ingredient is a computer. Some states do require a credit service organization bond or local business license. Learn more at CreditRepairCloud.com/all-states.

How Can I Make Money At Credit Repair?

Watch this free web training: CreditRepairCloud.com/FreeTraining.

How Much Money Can I Make?

Credit repair can be highly profitable, but it's hard work. This is not a get rich quick scheme. But if you have a head for business and are good with people, this is an awesome field. Here's a ROI calculator that will give you an idea on how lucrative a recurring revenue business can be: CreditRepairCloud.com/calculator.

How Much Should I Charge My Clients?

That's entirely up to you — but in this business, you might actually make more by charging less. Learn more at: http:// support.creditrepaircloud.com/knowledge-base/how-much-should-i-charge-my-clients and see our Pricing/ROI Calculator at www.creditrepaircloud.com/calculator.

Where Do I Get A Website?

If you don't have your own website, get one today at www.mycreditrepairsite.com.

How Do I Get Help With Credit Repair Cloud?

Just ask! We have free and fast support. We can also help you 1-on-1 by phone for free, just visit www.creditrepaircloud.com/support.

How Do I Get A Merchant Account For Credit Repair?

Visit www.creditrepaircloud.com/merchant.

Can I Charge Upfront Fees For Credit Repair?

The Credit Repair Organizations Act spells out how credit repair businesses may operate. Some states will want you to charge after work is done rather than before. How do credit repair businesses make money that way? In many cases, they do some work, and then they get paid for the work they've just done. They are being paid for "document processing" and "credit counseling" and not to "raise scores." They import a report and send off a round of letters (about 10 mins of work) and then they charge a "1st work fee." Then every month they send off another round of letters or click to update status of items that were removed (about five minutes of work) and they charge a monthly fee. This is why the monthly recurring model works so well for credit repair. There are additional state and federal laws to consider. For more information visit CreditRepairCLoud.com/all-states.

How Do I Increase Credit Scores?

By using the law in your favor. Read the first section of this book.

How Do I Get More Clients?

Watch this webinar: CreditRepairCloud.com/FreeTraining.

Who Orders The Credit Reports?

Your client orders their own reports. Have them sign up for credit monitoring. They can get all 3 reports and scores for $1. If you're a Credit Repair Cloud user, you'll see a list of compatible providers within our software under MY COMPANY>CREDIT MONITORING SERVICE.

Can I Order The Credit Reports For The Client?

No way, José! We asked some of the biggest credit repair firms and here's how they handle report ordering: Most companies have the client sign up for credit monitoring and then they have their client share the login details.

Does My Client's Score Suffer A Hit If He Orders His Own Report?

No. There's no hit to the score if the client is ordering their own reports.

I Can't Download My Free Credit Reports From The Credit Bureau Site!

Credit bureau websites are unfriendly. Their goal is to make money. We have no affiliation to the credit bureaus. We provide an easy link to their websites where you can order reports, but free reports from a bureau site are not useful, they will not have scores and they will not import into software. Encourage your client to sign up for (and maintain) a credit monitoring account for the entire period of the credit repair. This way you can both see the changes each month to the reports and scores. Credit monitoring is a necessary expense during credit repair.

Which Dispute Letter Do I Choose?

Always start in Wizard 3 and always start with a Round 1 letter, which is sent directly to the credit bureaus. This letter is always the same, so you don't need to worry about it. Just use the Default Round 1 Letter in the Credit Wizard for a quick send that will get your client's credit repair started (along with your revenue stream). For Round 2 (and higher) see page 79 for "Choosing a Dispute Letter."

How Many Items Can I Dispute At One Time?

We recommend that you send as few as possible and never more than five per month per bureau. This will keep your letters from being flagged as frivolous, which is something difficult to overcome. The exception would be if there's blatant identity theft with lots of bogus inquiries and new accounts. Always proceed with caution if you plan to dispute more than 5 items in a one month.

What Is The Statute Of Limitations For Debt Collection?

It varies by state. Click here for a full guide: https://www.creditrepaircloud.com/statute-of-limitations-sol-on-debt.

Who Signs And Sends The Dispute Letters?

In most cases an actual signature is not needed, but if you use Credit Repair Cloud, the client will choose a signature "font" that will automatically print with the letters. The credit repair business sends the letters on behalf of the client.

Do I Have To Let My Clients See Their Dispute Letters?

Yes! Trying to prevent your client from seeing the letters you're sending is actually illegal. You DO NOT have a choice in this matter! If you're sending letters on behalf of your clients, you MUST let the clients have access to them and know exactly what you're sending on their behalf, otherwise you're in violation of the law. CROA, the Credit Repair Organizations act states that the client must have access to anything sent on their behalf.

Should I Put Legalese Into My Dispute Letters?

In most cases, no. Credit dispute letters are sent "as if" they are from the client so this will definitely be a red flag unless the client is an attorney. The best dispute letters are very simple and very short and just state simple facts as concise as possible.

What Do I Include With The Dispute Letters?

With your Round 1 letter to the bureaus, always include a photo ID (like a driver's license), plus a proof of address (like a utility bill). If your client does not have a driver's license, they can use a state issued photo ID, a passport or a social security card. If your client doesn't have a utility bill that shows their current address, they can also use an insurance statement, bank statement, credit card bill or even a phone bill. You won't need to send these for the later rounds since you've already established in Round 1 that the disputes are indeed coming from the client.

Should I Send The Dispute Letters By Certified Mail?

Certified mail is not mandatory, but we do recommend it. Certified mail will give you a better paper trail and time stamps that prove exactly when the letter was sent. This often come in handy.

Why Send Everything By Snail Mail? Can't I Do This Online?

Snail mail is how credit repair works best. This is the same method used by the largest credit repair businesses in America who make hundreds of millions of dollars. You're being paid for a few minutes of work for document processing and sending letters. Spring for the envelope and the stamp.

How Do I Stop The Words "Credit Repair Cloud" And Your Url From Printing On My Letters?

You'll want to change the print settings in your web browser for that. It's very easy and there are instructions for this in the page of Credit Repair Cloud where you print out your letters.

What Happens After Round 1?

Round 2 of course! See the chapter for "Choosing a Dispute Letter." If you're using Credit Repair Cloud and you're in Round 2, choose the "Letter Finder" feature and it will help you to choose the perfect letter every time.

My Client Is Undermining My Work By Applying For Credit And Keeping High Balances. What Should I Do?

Give them awesome service and educate them. See the chapter called "Educate Your Clients."

How Do I Do Email Marketing?

We're not an email marketing platform, so email marketing is something you will do on your own outside of our Credit Repair Cloud software. Be careful because there are many laws about email marketing and spam. The company that is most credit repair friendly is ActiveCampaign.com.

Should I Buy Ads?

This is generally not necessary. You can get more clients for free by following the steps in our Free Web Training: CreditRepairCloud.com/freetraining.

What Are The Laws Of Starting A Credit Repair Business?

Folks operate credit repair businesses in every state, but each state is a little different. Check with your state and consult an attorney. We are a software company. We can't give you legal advice. You can see the laws for each state here on our site: CreditRepairCloud.com/all-states.

Do I Need A Bond?

You might. A few states do require them — but if one is required, you only pay a fraction of the cost (usually just 2-3% of the total bond amount). Visit Bonds Express at www.bondsexpress.com/credit-services-organization-bond/ to see if one is required in your state. They can answer any questions you may have about bonds.

What Should I Know About Compliance?

Don't make deceptive claims. This is one of the biggest mistakes a new credit repair business owner will make. Never make false claims or guarantees. Credit repair cannot work that way. Be honest. You cannot promise a score increase in 30 days or removal of everything negative. But you can explain how the credit repair process works. Give some education to the client on how they can speed up the process by not applying for new debt and paying bills down; you can also give some examples of stats on your other clients, for example: "Our average client sees 5 to 10 items removed in the first three months, but all clients are different." If the goal is to grow and scale your business, take it slow and always be honest and transparent.

Ask your clients which items to dispute. This is another very common mistake made by new credit repair companies. You cannot dispute everything. Consult with the client and only dispute what the client tells you to dispute.

Here are two methods for this:

Simple method: Evaluate the report with the client. The client should tell you which items are accurate and which items are not.

More complex method: Use our "client's choice" module. Once that is enabled (in My Company>Portal>Client's Choice, the client must make the choices after the report is imported).

Make sure you have a contract in place before you start adding clients. It should include:

- Your company name and address
- Your payment terms for services
- A clear description of the services you will provide
- Any guarantees or refund policies (if offered)
- Authorization for Credit Repair Action (this is like a limited power of attorney)
- The expected time it will take to achieve results (estimates are fine)
- A copy of the FTC's "Consumer Credit File Rights"
- A cancellation notice giving clients 3 business days after signing to legally cancel

Also see the Federal and State laws here on our site: CreditRepairCloud.com/all-states.

Credit Repair Cloud, Training & Certification

Now That You've Read This Book

I hope you found it motivating and informative. I'd like to invite you to try out Credit Repair Cloud.

What is Credit Repair Cloud?

Credit Repair Cloud is the world's first cloud-based credit repair software. It powers most of the credit repair industry. It's designed to help you to start, run, and grow a profitable credit repair business. Import credit reports, generate letters with a click, manage your clients, your team and your affiliates with ease. Try it free at CreditRepairCloud.com.

Our customers are credit repair companies, finance professionals, attorneys, realtors, CPA's, auto dealers, Fortune 500 Companies and home based entrepreneurs with a mission to change lives.

It's the world's most affordable startup. All you need is a computer and a passion to change lives.

How successful Credit Repair Companies make millions

- If you keep your existing "paying" clients happy
- And you add a few more clients each month

Your revenue will grow **larger** every month!

The Millionaire's Club

The Millionaires Club exists to provide recognition to those who took action, change a lot of lives, and grossed $1,000,000 revenue using Credit Repair Cloud. Many of our Millionaire users started from nothing. Many were homeless. We share their stories as inspiration that anyone with hard work and focus can get massive success in credit repair. More than just the money, they are changing thousands of lives.

Meet some of our Millionaires

Ashley Massengill
Quit her job at the Post Office

Arron Clarke
Went from homeless to hero

Deunka Alston
Young mother who wanted a flexible business

Serge Bagdasarov
Nearly lost his life, now he changes lives

Andre Coakley
Had enough of the mortgage industry

Jose Rodriguez
Turned his challenges into successes

Tracy Arnett
Was a victim of ID theft and now help others

Samuel Naquin
Left real estate business to help home buyers

Seth Mitchel
Overcame adversity and emerged a winner

Jeff Rubins
Loves helping people to reach their dreams

Abraham Matyas
Wanted to change lives in his close community

Derrick Harper Sr.
Started by helping his friends in the Air Force

At the time of this writing, nearly 50 people have made this exclusive list, with more coming in every month. To hear their inspiring stories visit:
www.CreditRepairCloud.com/Success-Stories